A Notebook of Clouds

A Notebook of Ridges

A Notebook of Clouds
by Pierre Chappuis
(translated from the French by John Taylor)

A Notebook of Ridges
by John Taylor

ODD VOLUMES

OF

THE FORTNIGHTLY REVIEW

LES BROUZILS

2019

Copyright © 2018 Pierre Chappuis for the original French texts of *A Notebook of Clouds* and *The Preliminary Notebook*, and for translations into all other languages.

English Translation Copyright © 2018 John Taylor for Pierre Chappuis's *A Notebook of Clouds* and *The Preliminary Notebook*.

Copyright © 2018 John Taylor for *A Notebook of Ridges* and "The Word and the Stream."
978-0-9991365-4-6

Pierre Chappuis's *Un cahier de nuages* was first published in 1988 in a limited edition by the Éditions Thierry Bouchard, with five etchings by André Siron, and then in 1989 by the Éditions Le Feu de nuict, founded by Pierre Voélin and Frédéric Wandelère. The excerpts from *The Preliminary Notebook* are unpublished in French and appear here for the first time in English.

Excerpts from John Taylor's *A Notebook of Ridges* appeared in a French translation by the author in *La Revue de belles-lettres* (No. 2, 2017), as part of a special feature on Pierre Chappuis. With warm thanks to the editor, Marion Graf. The poetic sequence "The Word and the Stream" first appeared in *The Bitter Oleander* (Volume 24, No. 1, Spring 2018), as part of a special feature on John Taylor. With warm thanks to the editor, Paul B. Roth.

Odd Volumes
The Fortnightly Review
Editorial office: Château le Ligny
2 rue Georges Clémenceau 85260
Les Brouzils France.
http://fortnightlyreview.co.uk/odd-volumes/
email info@fortnightlyreview.co.uk

iv

An Initial Explanation

This dual project gradually took shape after I had translated several books by Pierre Chappuis and Seagull Books had published them together in 2016 as *Like Bits of Wind: Selected Poetry and Poetic Prose 1974-2013*. While preparing that manuscript, I had translated excerpts of *A Notebook of Clouds*, but I eventually left them out of the Seagull selection. There are formal differences between this book and the collections of verse poetry and poetic prose texts that make up *Like Bits of Wind*. In *A Notebook of Clouds*, there are indeed verse poems and poetic prose texts, but also notes, fragments, quotations, word play, and even meteorological facts. The various genres are organized into a different kind of coherent sequence. The book forms a whole that must be read as such.

As I was translating the rest of *A Notebook of Clouds*, the very form of Pierre Chappuis's book suggested, with increasing insistency, that I embark upon a similar project. A word kept surfacing in my mind: "ridge." The word had fascinated me ever since my childhood in the flatlands of Iowa. Initially as a kind of experiment, I thus jotted down memories, ideas, and emotions that cropped up whenever I thought about the word. (I should add that I have long lived in a part of Western France where, as in Iowa, ridges are rare.) I began to fill a small notebook, often while riding on trains. Not long afterwards, a two-week stay in the Alps, near the village of Névache and the Valley of the Claré, enabled me to add some specific perceptions of ridges and remember still others, notably in the Rocky Mountains. Whereupon emerged *A Notebook of Ridges* as well as "The Word and the Stream", which I have appended to the former.

As Pierre Chappuis and I were putting our double manuscript together, he came across a second notebook devoted to the same subject. He had long thought that it had been lost. So I have translated excerpts from what he calls the "Preliminary Notebook for the *Notebook of Clouds*, 1979-1984." He stipulates that the "impressions and reflections in it make up only raw material." As the reader will see, the texts function as forethoughts and even afterthoughts, though they were written beforehand, to his *Notebook of Clouds*.

—J. T.

Table of Contents

A Notebook of Clouds 1

from The Preliminary Notebook 57

A Notebook of Ridges 79

The Word and the Stream...123

Notes 141

A NOTEBOOK OF CLOUDS

...land and cloud, far and near, sun and dream...
Hugo von Hofmannsthal

*Nighttime clouds
spread out like a tablecloth*

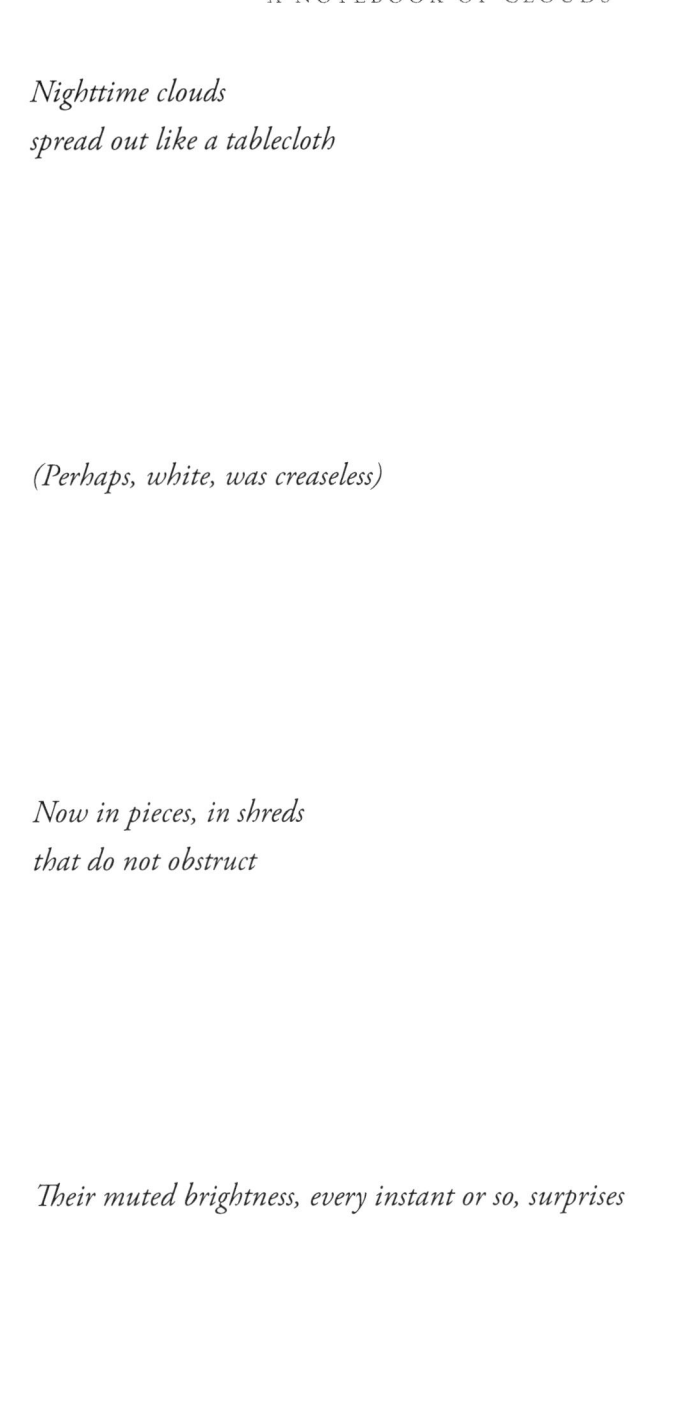

(Perhaps, white, was creaseless)

*Now in pieces, in shreds
that do not obstruct*

Their muted brightness, every instant or so, surprises

Stendhal: "If I had the slightest knowledge of meteorology, I wouldn't take so much pleasure, on some days, in watching clouds fly by and in delighting in the magnificent palaces or gigantic monsters that they represent for my imagination. I once observed a Swiss chalet shepherd who spent three hours, his arms crossed in front of him, contemplating the covered peaks of the Jungfrau *(!)*. For him, it was a kind of music. My ignorance often nears me to that shepherd's state."

Clouds, cloudlets——"Stilled beneath the oppressive cloud"; "Her head on her arm and her arm on the cloudlet"—and a thousand other cloudy nuances, strictly speaking, for which we lack words and which are ever renewed—O memory!—and resemble each other. Hazes and fogs; curls, twists, wandering orchards or bundles often grayer than white and—rambling clouds, ramblers—hobbling along the roads. "I love clouds. . . passing clouds. . . over there. . . faraway. . . the marvelous clouds. . ."

Not without cheating—if to the letter also means *in reality* (untruthfulness, the very ambiguity of poetry)—literally, as long as it takes to read a book: to be in the clouds.

Larks, swallows, an airplane, a dove as well as the shades of ancestors vanish into clouds from which anyone recklessly managing by his own means alone to rise as high will fatally fall. Like the hermit of Kume whose talent for levitation acquired through deprivation and fasting was annihilated in one blow, according to the Japanese legend, when he spotted a washerwoman's bare arms and legs at the edge of the water.

In the same *Idle Hours* by Urabe Kenko: "A hermit, whose name escapes me, said: *Nothing binds me to this world anymore. I'm only affected by the fleeting beauty of the seasons in the sky.* This sentiment earns my sympathy."

"Fragrant haze, a chignon of damp cloud," goes a line of verse by Du Fu. But as these "dawn clouds in pink satin, evening clouds in red brocade, clouds of every hour" change their names as often as their colors and shapes, Chinese clouds have an exceptional variety of terms.

Shelley speaks of unbuilding the "blue dome of air" that has been built up by the sun and the wind. However, as something completely different (is it a man already doomed by his illness that utters these words?), "the grandiose architecture of the clouds leaves me with my chaos."

Little by little, a *Poetic Atlas of Clouds* could be put together as the equally international counterpart of the *Cloud Atlas* of the World Meteorological Organization. A geography in motion giving rise to exchanges between it and us —"the room abandoned to the clouds. . . the clouds left to the sea. . .," indeed finding a foundation here—"On the grass of the clouds a plowshare of light."

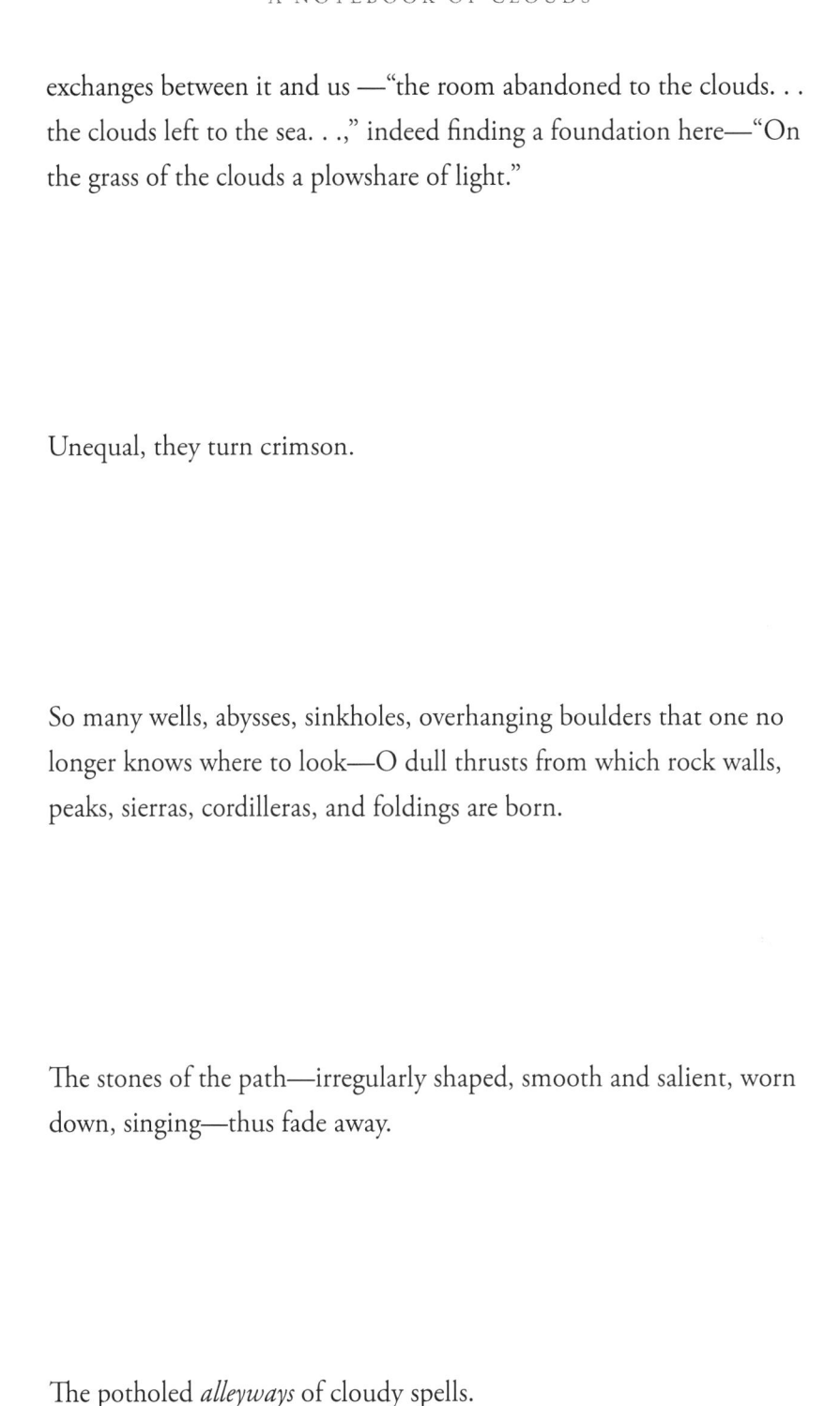

Unequal, they turn crimson.

So many wells, abysses, sinkholes, overhanging boulders that one no longer knows where to look—O dull thrusts from which rock walls, peaks, sierras, cordilleras, and foldings are born.

The stones of the path—irregularly shaped, smooth and salient, worn down, singing—thus fade away.

The potholed *alleyways* of cloudy spells.

Cast to the four winds. Vast umbels. Feathers flurrying into powder.

Mutely shouting themselves hoarse.

Extending from a gap ripped open from below in the thick layer massed over the land, and with their teeth turned upwards, a ridge bristling with spruce trees.

Adrift—extreme, crepuscular.

Half-melted on the tongue, still bearing clarity.

The front of the ice field right there, in sight, like a boundary wall.

As I open my notebook to record it, once again my object eludes me. A different sky once again, in the blink of an eye.

(But does *drawing a blank cloud* mean failing?)

Upside down, in summer, in the blue,
in an infinitely fragmented plain,

may he follow, as he wishes, paths that break off only to begin again, a little further on, along hedges, fields, or wastelands.

Cold front clouds

a front railing
an aching frontal bone
a front lever

Cloudy to overcast. Wednesday and Thursday: same kind of weather.

Plentiful, crumpled, pushed aside, rough drafts clutter up the sky—the blank page routed.

However, the page doesn't write itself. *It's out there, up there, up in the air.*

Decorative foliage, moldings, festoons of flowers or fruit, wreaths.

The cloud cover thickens.

These heavy clouds (as one says: a heavy stomach, a heavy head) hovering like a ceiling, crushing, imprisoning—this stuffiness, this numbing mugginess—no.

. . . Flapping in the wind like frenzied fringes; in flight, as light as birds. Or whipped, full of gaps, soon undone.

(In praise of dissipation.)

Clot swollen into a mountain.

Bound to the earth: *cloud*, akin to *clod*, from a word originally meaning "hill."
Mountains drifting.

Unstable land dwellers: from clod to clot, bale, bundle: nomads' bundles.

In places, depending on the mending, more or less clear patches get longer, rounder, are resorbed; creases, festoons hardly formed are taken back into the mass. Holes close up again, or the dough sticking to the rolling pin rises, at once flayed and gluey. A little flour makes it firm and fresh again.
Resumption of the stretching; distorting and reshaping in all directions.

Quenelles, eggs, cauliflowers, lost in white sauce.

Gathered back up in haste before the rainfall, sheets seemingly heaped up just like that in a laundry basket.

Extravagant rags!

Seeds. Breadcrumbs. Semolina.
Road and peaks are sparkling.

Changing; variable.

Would require constant revision, from instant to instant: different groupings of words, different words, different sentences, null and void in less time than it takes to write them down.

Like poached eggs solidified as they are bursting open.
Or blancmanges, rice pudding, floating islands.

Onto the very daylight (the glare, the screen of morning) opens a window of fog.

The trace of an ancient Roman road with unequal, disjointed paving stones (with no ruts hollowed into them) ends up fading into a blur.

Elsewhere, an azure thoroughfare (doesn't Strasbourg have a *Blue Cloud Street?*) snakes its way between facades needing a facelift.

Willingly pulled hither and thither, ready for anything, a simple accumulation of drifting elements more apt—even if similar, even if following each other—to dismantle a sentence than to solder it together, as uncertain of its conclusion as its form, the enumeration still could—or can—become murkier, like a stormy sky, or, on the contrary, ease up, thin out, come undone, prone to variable air currents.

Lends the support only of its instability.

Dispossession (a path to plenitude?) more than abundance, its calling lies in the emptiness that threatens it, has seeped inside it everywhere, not in the whole that will bring it back together.

Peak or picture rail, like a fabulous palace in ruins whose walls, whose inner walls with their faded frescoes, rise into emptiness.
Like the petrified hem of a high wave.

Its brightness threatening, a great wall of foam—impalpable tidal wave—doesn't move.

Motionless stormy furor.

Like a tidal wave: unobstructed, soldiers are marching upon us (from the depths of history) in rows so tight that the crests of their white-plumed helmets seem to touch.

$C_h C_i$ (fib. int.) 4 p.m. before a cold front.

(Keep a *diary* of clouds? Preferably, on a few loose sheets of paper. . .)

Their hair tousled, pale with rage, fated for a fine tussle, yet soon they fizzle out.

Are no longer what they were.

Toward evening, here they are puffed up once again, red-faced, their crests shaking histrionically, rather comically, however terrifying their confrontation could be if they by chance go into action.

Taking the cloud as it comes, indeed, in its variety, its regrets, sometimes in pieces, sometimes steady and smooth, the only chance to grasp it—in mouthfuls, in handfuls.
Without worrying about whatever might fly off madly in all directions, everything that the winds will push this way.

Like entangled noodles which, softened and whirling, would come undone little by little in the cooking water.

(". . .thicker than vermicelli, shorter than. . .")
Mitres transmuted into salt deposits transmuted into vast cotton plantations.

Nipple-hilled; sandy.

Tables or seracs, anvils, hoods, mustaches or even (across the Atlantic, in Quebec) "cow tails," "windy feet."

Nimbus, cumulus, forward, fast!

Forming flocks, taken up in a rush or a chase—*fibratus, flocus, castellanus* and, as to the variety, *intortus, vertebratus*, etc.—but other words are needed, everyday speech is needed for clouds—

scientific or colloquial, arachnidan, jagged, gossamer, wafers, or sheep huddled against each other, or indeed roan horses, mottled horses, little gray and blond buckskin horses
with a single disorderly movement, ride on, fast, fast before the feast is over!

Steady or brief, more or less in quick succession, unheard sounds seemingly calling out to each other within wide blue margins.

Fluctuating arpeggios, hummed.

Like sounds that would not be heard. . . Like unheard-of sounds. . .

Suddenly (barely the time to turn one's head) it's no longer through high autumn pastures that I walk, but (without touching the ground) through an entirely white expanse.

It rises

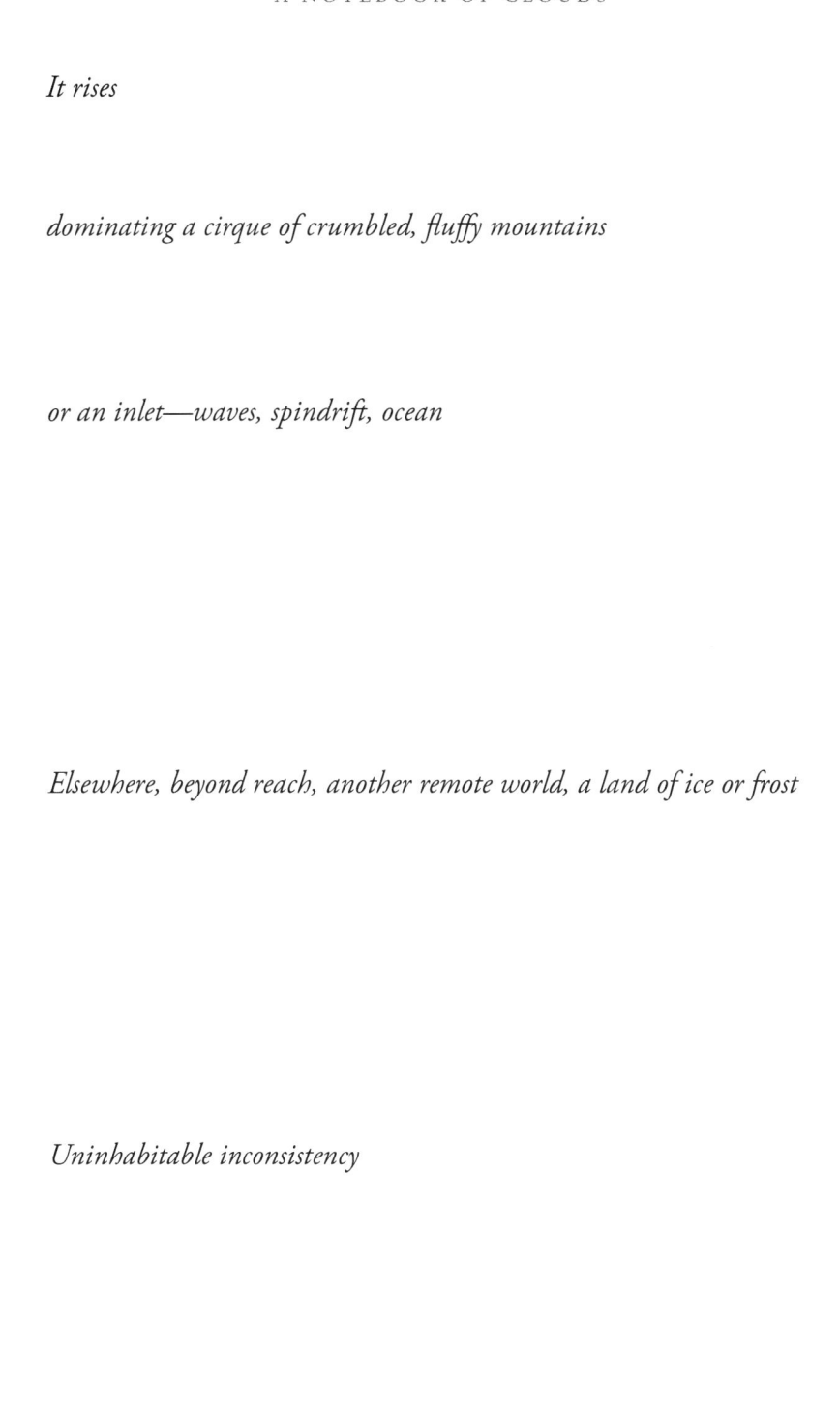

dominating a cirque of crumbled, fluffy mountains

or an inlet—waves, spindrift, ocean

Elsewhere, beyond reach, another remote world, a land of ice or frost

Uninhabitable inconsistency

EVER HALTED, FROM THE ONSET

Smooth, this morning, a vertical sea

Neither top nor bottom. Wherever the gaze wanders (does it wander? it blends), it enters, has already entered, has lost its way, sinks in; exact and nil

vanishes, like a lost-head nail drowned in the expanse

In the meantime (no longer time) clear and gloomy, between rain and sunlight (ever halted)

Upside-down sea; vapors; a moving and stable abode; haze reigning everywhere

A PAST THAT WOULD NOT WEIGH DOWN

Ancestral
Fruits of chance (transfers and sharing out); arbitrarily dividing up pastures

Broken down into shadings of color, collapsed here or there

(Smudges, smeared lines: similarly flecked with fleecy clouds, many gray wisps)

Every year, stone by stone, they are set back upright

This is how they cross the naked summer

Edges running across the entire plateau like foundations (but of enormous constructions) given back to the open air by archeologists

Mountain blurred by the wind

UNMOVING

Unmoving, without settling down

Abrupt
chipped

—But
of landslide, ejected matter
nothing!—

Horizon's barrier on the move

DAMASK HORIZON

Rains, winds (this noon with its hung-out washing, blinds, mobile panels), rising waves, water so close to daylight and violent, cloudy, foamy

and the fledged arrow (a hot iron pressed down, a crease), the hazy wing—engulfed just as soon—stops the altered gaze, luminously, which, all coming and going (greyhound unleashed across the fields), irons, smooths out the silky selvage, the white lamé headband, whiteness that the whiteness brings to life (hardly a crease, itinerant, iterative, a gather)

rain, winds, water like ploughed rows marching along, cloud or shore in the distance leave me all alone

MUSICAL BELL

Like sounds beyond earshot, they intermingle, extend or, being brief, call out to each other from afar in an expanse

a margin of silence

Morning, relentlessly, from one gap to the other, is rebuilt

The boat, no

but its wake
luminous fold, overseas trench

Lively, with a sharpened blade

Yet it frays at the edges

A nicked blade would have slashed roughly through the azure above the horizon, soon making room for a freshly whitewashed wall on which white ostriches would strut along.

Or, in the distance, in open country, rises an enormous, half-demolished, baroque basilica made of gleaming marble; immediately recognized as the goal of the trip, but—surprise!—it's the basilica that is coming in our direction.

There exist *accessory* clouds that form a bonnet, or a veil, or drift below a thicker layer.

Goethe's stupid advice to Caspar David Friedrich to undertake a genuine, well thought-out study of clouds in order to paint them better.

Is not enclosed, a garden, Eden.

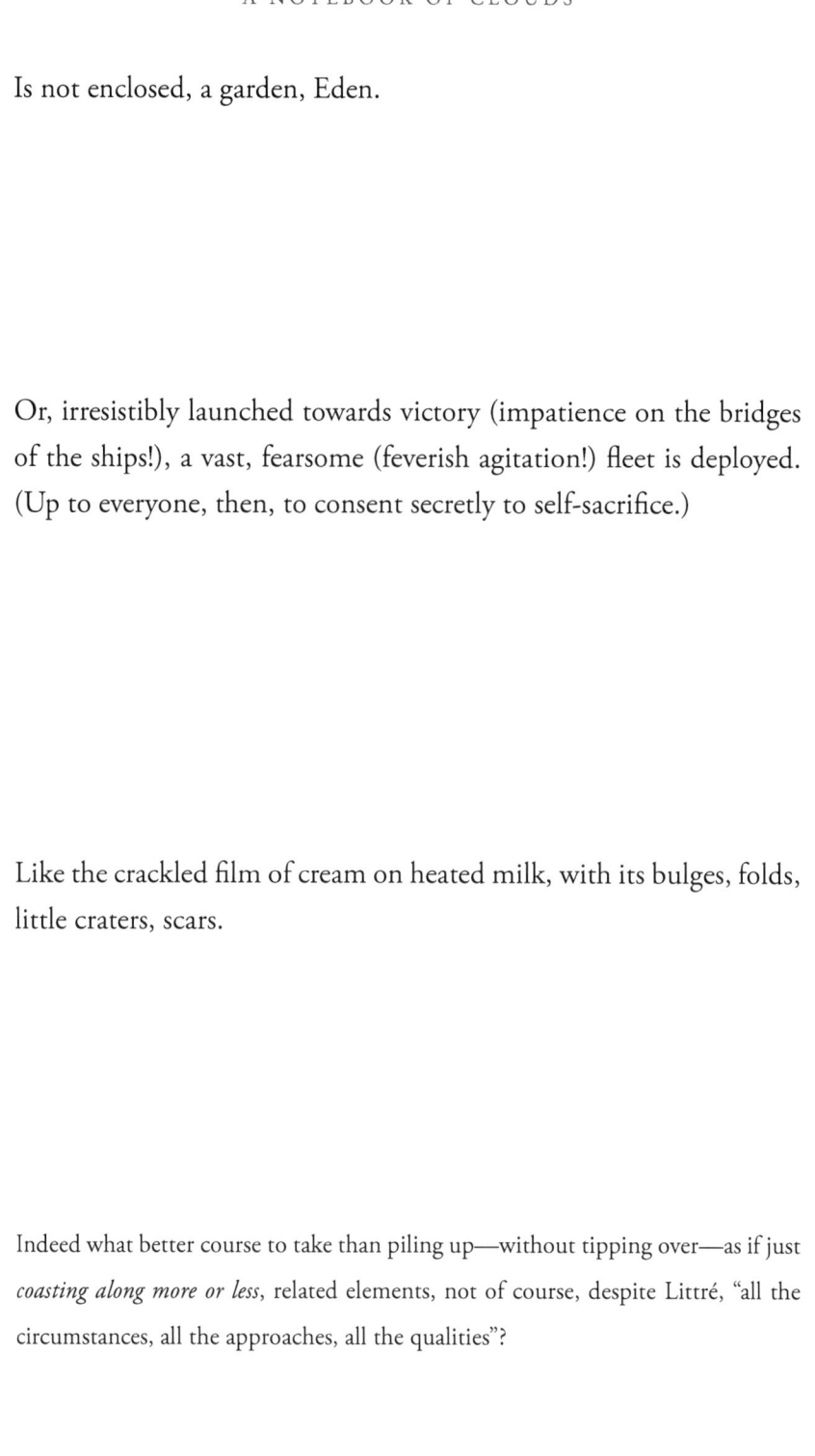

Or, irresistibly launched towards victory (impatience on the bridges of the ships!), a vast, fearsome (feverish agitation!) fleet is deployed. (Up to everyone, then, to consent secretly to self-sacrifice.)

Like the crackled film of cream on heated milk, with its bulges, folds, little craters, scars.

Indeed what better course to take than piling up—without tipping over—as if just *coasting along more or less*, related elements, not of course, despite Littré, "all the circumstances, all the approaches, all the qualities"?

But how to ensure that the pleasure of the reader who is free, every time, to follow his whims as if it were the *perpetual present* of a changing sky, does not result from an elaboration (leaving no trace), from hard work, from a sometimes uneasy polishing?

Instead of becoming one with the summer these past few days, with the heat, with a sky whose purity is rare, to stumble over the slightest word (be it out of enthusiasm)—what a constraint!

Break-offs that are offset, clouds of clouds, by parentheses.

Sandy shores of dream—dream-sand shores—Nelly Sachs's unforgettable word *Traumsandufern*, which has no equivalent for us, soft like sand and like dream—*dreamy shores of sand*—all at once, a blending of words and senses, closing up every gap.

Sand like dream, O shores, O clouds!

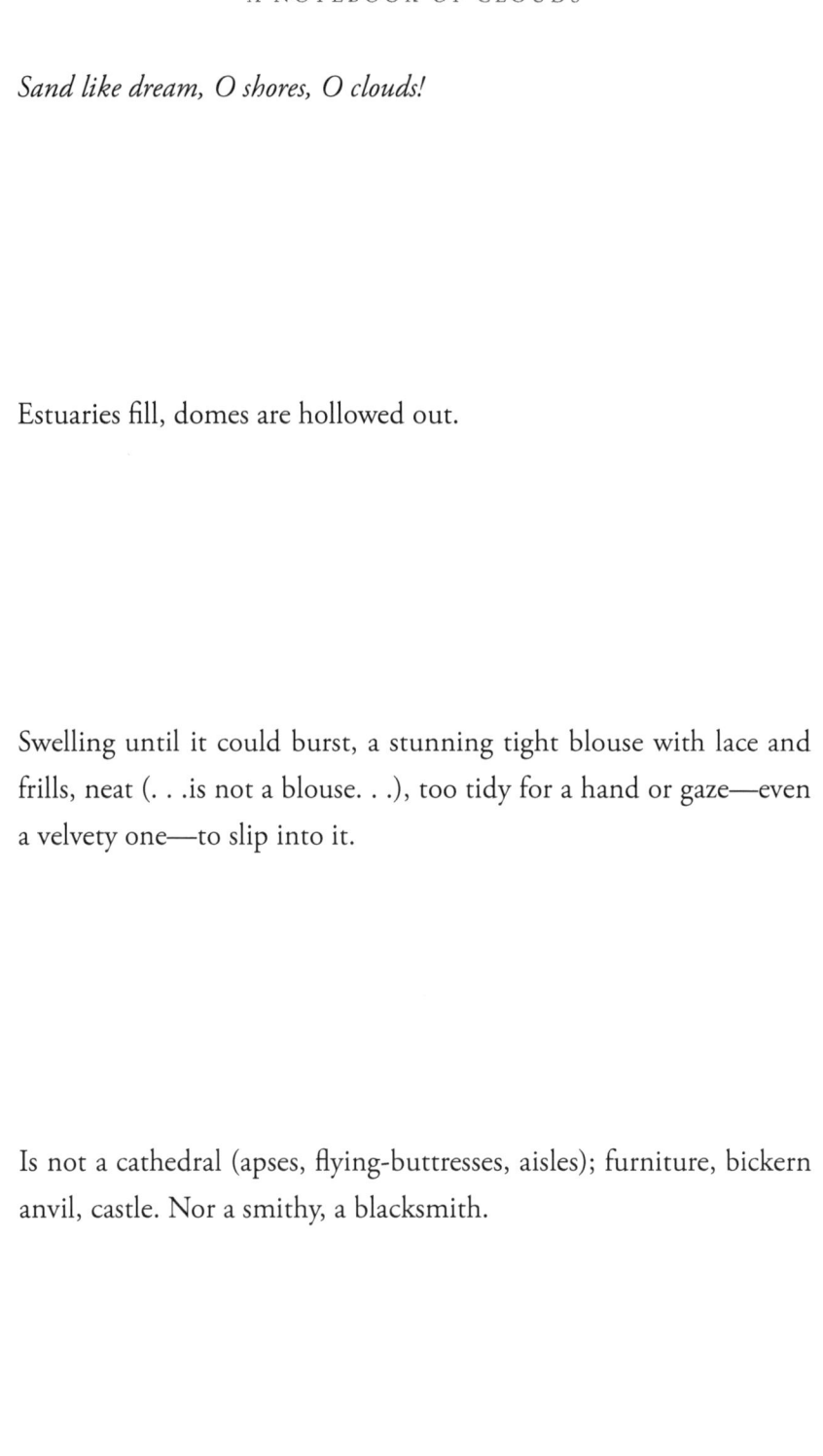

Estuaries fill, domes are hollowed out.

Swelling until it could burst, a stunning tight blouse with lace and frills, neat (. . .is not a blouse. . .), too tidy for a hand or gaze—even a velvety one—to slip into it.

Is not a cathedral (apses, flying-buttresses, aisles); furniture, bickern anvil, castle. Nor a smithy, a blacksmith.

Cloud castles
like
card castles

or castles in Spain

Is not an unfurling of sails, nor wall coverings, nor oriflammes.

Nor does it fling itself, having lingered, into the jaws of an eager devourer.

Ashy forests show the way with clearings that overlap before canceling each other out.

Dunes as well, remote announcement of worlds in gestation.

Wealthy with so many kinds of absence, where are we?

Comings and goings amid snow-draped pines as if amid the disorder of a transit camp, among a people of clouds.

Canopy, ceiling, pergola.

Banderoles, banners, printed calicos and other kinds of fabric made of muslin (cloth from Mosul) are unfurled—or, to travel a little, of satin (Shandong), of shantung silk—nearer to us cretonne, mull.

Right out of the Bagdad of the *Thousand and One Nights*, an enormous flying baldachin with heavy curtains, with twisted columns, struggles to rise above all the bedlam-like coming and going.

Simon says

keep sitting

stand up and be a cloud

If it were possible, every melodic line drowned out in the mixing and remixing of material swept along, ground down, stirred up (sometimes marvelously calmed down), split into islets, into strophes, to find, if it were possible, the equivalent of *prose* (so to speak) in fusion—eruptive and connected—of Béla Bartók from whom sometimes tends to emerge, timid, unsure, barely out of its gangue, an unheard-of song crystallized just as it is born.

An ode or, disorder settling in, a horde is unleashed.
A herd in tattered clothes just as well.

Even as late-autumn leaves and twigs rolled along by the waves end up forming on the shore a dark instable bulge marking the water limit,

so, sweeping along above our heads, clouds gather on the horizon.

In any event, a vast cleaning operation is going on.

Island, mountain

the cold, the air of the open sea
the hirsute sea

Hobbling along (the ground gives way) between *verse* and *prose*, resisting any kind of stiffening (perhaps illusorily: "If it's formless, he gives it as formless"), hopping from one foot to the other (like limping, skipping along after the fashion of a junior-high-school student skipping school, with his nose in the air), no longer knowing which way I should turn.

Ploughed fields: winter aflame (or beneath our feet, sky and clouds) gradually licking the ground.

The shadow makes a ravine of the parallel ridges on which daylight's cutting edge is being sharpened.

Is neither frozen ground nor. . .

In a heap of stones disturbed by the slightest breeze, an aerial well opens.

Bright cloud masses uncover at times, through a gap—still hazy?—a snowy summit.

With a tremendous din, the pillars of Hercules would be shattered.

(And the sea, the sea. . .)

Or they are pillars of smoke rising above some devastated city soon to be swallowed up?

(The desolation, the ceaseless moaning of the sea. . .)

Disaster, cataclysm: shame at tossing out such rash remarks about which the sky, even temporarily, by no means darkens.
(Writing, that futile act.)

Jaws closed on emptiness.

Uneven, chalky, incongruous (which nearby lumps of plaster are trampled on?), footsteps fade away in the rain.

A grayish breakup that will not last.

Sometimes, before the storm, they're so shiny white (an acidic transparence) that, seemingly (like sherbet bitten into rashly), they *give you a toothache.*

Pressing against each other, overturned... "so that one face / is effaced by the stroke that the other face effaces"... but, despite the whirlwinds, the sudden changes, ever (may it be the same here) in the movement, in the coherence of the moment.

Dark mane, beautiful dapple-gray coat—and not for an instant does the fieriness slacken.

Unmoving, in broad daylight

So high, among armfuls of frost

Burst open

Visible on the surface, upside down, the more or less worn or buried rows of an ancient theater surrounded by gentle hills.

At least once, to carry myself higher. But I remain nailed to the ground.

Opens out an alpine lake surrounded by narrow trails—parallel, immemorial—hollowed out along the slope by livestock that regularly pass by.

Luminous sphincter.

Was shafting . . (my astonishment, probably barely beyond the age of reading children's books, when I came across—where? in what poem?—such a verb that seemed impossible to use in the present tense, yet that has ever since remained associated with certain luxuriously, sumptuously heavy skies). . . the sun (indeed, today!) shafts its rays sideways between lambrequins and twisted columns.

In a halo of sunlight, of rain, a sheet-metal roof shines, white fire on high

Blue itself

The moving ridge, from there, stands out differently.

Debussy: *Clouds*. Ligeti: *Clocks and Clouds*.

Clouds, baroque skies. A beam as if projected downwards from the lamp of a cupola or the top of an altarpiece in order to envelop, in its fan of light, dresses, drapes, ornaments, a whole joyous hustle and bustle with revered cherubs, saints, a perhaps too exuberant feast, an ascension or a tumbling down—the chosen soaring upwards, the damned vainly clutching at each other.

Among the artificial boulders, grottos, and fountains, tritons and naiads are cavorting, pushing each other with gusto, somersaulting.

In a burst of energy that is renewed every single instant, horses, their nostrils dilated, are neighing, roused by incessant leaps of foam.

Gray and pink, clear-colored, swollen like sails, they head for the open sea above Dutch plains and villages.

Or, with quietude and calamity in equilibrium, Poussin's soothing, deceiving, architecture.

Yet do I prefer Guardi with his skies mixed with colors, with his blended clouds? Or—theater and female impersonators in a perpetual carnival, be it celestial—Tiepolo's fleeting hazes?

The same whirlwinds impetuously sweep off fields and sky, and peasants at work wouldn't know how to make serene again he who, by painting, only deepens—dizziness, bedazzlement—his own torment.

Turner and his "atmospheric impressions." Or in Johan Christian Dahl's many sky *studies* (endless studies. . .) as well: the free shimmering of color.

Vestiges of dawns—a trail of white footprints, indeed—along the slope, down among the hedges, as the wind blows.

Amid April ash where a thousand embers are glowing (a vast, very vast apple orchard), wanders an orchard of clouds.

August 1975-August 1985

As if, scattered to the wind, the notes of a flute

Then the song fades away

Stone. A windowpane perhaps

As if clotted

A raffia cloth suspended over emptiness

from The Preliminary Notebook

31 July 1979

a cloud orchard

vanishes, in the West, opens out (large coves, inlets, a beach) almost, shining through, a Symbolist or Pre-Raphaelite sky

large coves, inlets
sand dunes

tissue paper

a screen, no, a breach
not that either
no more screen than breach

there, where every word is not resorbed, but resolved

also what *is not*

is not a garden. . . is not Eden, paradise, is not closed,

even as a cathedral, even as an edifice, is not closed

is   a white city so far
                                  it vanishes in the haze
                                  watermark
                                  (white on white)

now, it's like an awning—
a panel drawn across the end of an afternoon

                                  —and the light enters
the room
                      (outside, inside
identical)

awning-panel—hardly legible between the folds, the pattern of a piece of lacework

      and the room (and the conversation)
      is also blank,
      and the clothes

      (you, me, the beach in the distance)
of those who stand there
exchange rare words

vanishes as time goes by (but this can no longer be said)
takes it out on the branches

a poem that would destroy itself at the same time as it builds itself up, that would lose its form at the same time as it took on a form.

like a ball of yarn (indeed, what other word?), a ball of noodles which, little by little, in the cooking water, comes undone

a ringlet

like a tangle of noodles which, little by little, in the cooking water, comes undone

"Noodles are thicker than angel hair pasta, shorter than spaghetti. They are full, as opposed to macaroni. Noodles with sauce, au gratin, with cheese." A dictionary: what a marvelous book

but the noodle (what a noodle !) is not "worn well."

stretches, gets pierced, gathers together, can be shared!
Chewing gum, bubblegum.

in slabs, balls, tiny balls, meatballs, filaments, tidbits, a jumble, cornmeal, bits, scraps (the shape thereof), packets, abandoned in mid-air, broken down

(white breadcrumbs)

in seeds (the shape thereof), pearls, as powder! (the route, the sky, are getting powdery)

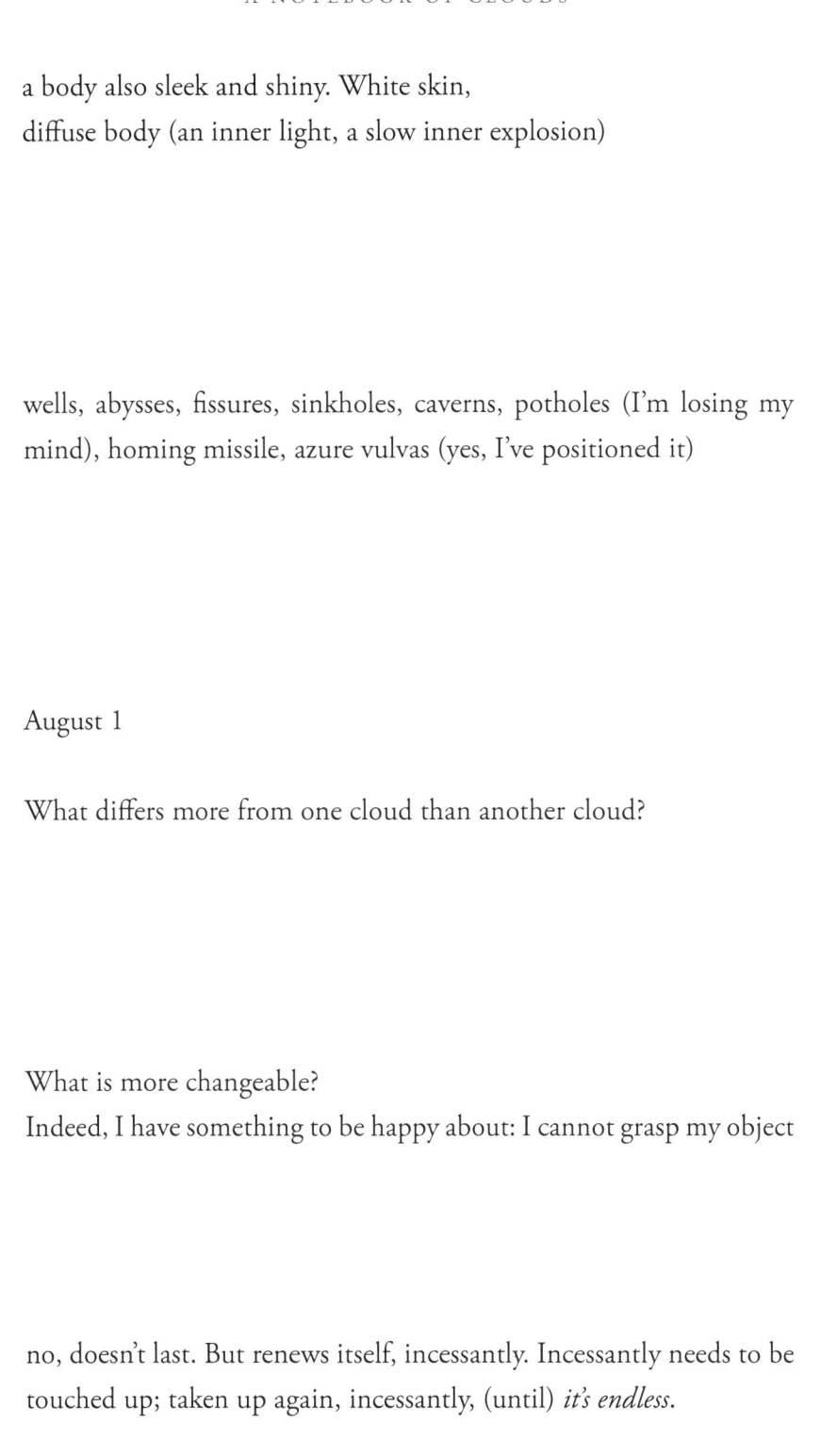

a body also sleek and shiny. White skin,
diffuse body (an inner light, a slow inner explosion)

wells, abysses, fissures, sinkholes, caverns, potholes (I'm losing my mind), homing missile, azure vulvas (yes, I've positioned it)

August 1

What differs more from one cloud than another cloud?

What is more changeable?
Indeed, I have something to be happy about: I cannot grasp my object

no, doesn't last. But renews itself, incessantly. Incessantly needs to be touched up; taken up again, incessantly, (until) *it's endless*.

always already surpassed

surpassed, at the very moment when I write it down (sometimes evolving definitely—the sky gradually—cleared, or, on the contrary, filling with clouds—or, sometimes, changing back to the same sky.

by bits or bunches
by stacks or snatches

already surpassed. . . what has no end
(what remains hungry at the end!)
what has no end, what goes on the contrary from its end, accumulating
(to accumulate, indeed: *cumulus*)
crumpled, wadded-up first drafts
scattered about, spilling out of the wastepaper basket,
invading desk and rug,
goes, on the contrary, from its end if its end
its only end is the blank page
(the only true, impossible "response" to the cloudy sky—
but no, this is still a theoretical viewpoint)

This is about, and not about, clouds.
This is both about them, in their presence, and *only* them,
[but I will never reach them]
and about the text to "build up,"
about *words* doing their best to *respond* to them

It is about parallel ways of functioning,
but it is also as much about real clouds as about cloudy skies in paintings

thus about images, thus about *playing with references* (and interferences)

but then be careful not to drain away the contents of the *object* (clouds), not to take it, any longer, initially, in its evidentness, not to use it any longer—as it were—except *allegorically*

that it be nothing any more than *playing* (with *ideas*).

All this is unclear. Everything is a matter of relations, of associations, an *object* is alive to the extent that it arouses a similar playing with references (and the *subject* is alive in this way as well)—may, simply stated, it not become *categorical* research, a biased choice. This is the danger of a NOTEBOOK devoted to a given "subject matter," there is something deliberate about it, something chilling, and this is perhaps why I had never written one, never attempted to write one until, to be precise, and a little by chance, four years ago, because an old notebook was lying around, never attempted to write one apropos of clouds. And the idea of a *Notebook of Clouds* filled out in a few days, or almost so, but abandoned, has haunted me ever since. A *Notebook* is very different from a *little pocket notebook* in which anything and everything is recorded, which exists, practically speaking, and is *under way*, to favor a piece of paper that one is not going to lose. Here, I had barely begun yesterday when I already sensed the notebook as a constraint—something *made ready*—: also, as I was *readying*, this morning, to take up my work once again, sitting at my desk, *settled in*, I had to escape, somehow fascinated as I was by the *lake*—its movement a kind of vocation of whiteness, like an underlying whiteness, barely surfacing.

[. . .]

A notebook thus presupposes, if not an outline, at least an intention. The text is born only by surprise, unexpectedly; subsequently, perhaps the work is, apparently, more or less pursued. The notebook destroys the conditions of emergence that it should encourage. I sense it a little like this, even as, already, instead of noting down anything and everything, I sense I am already in a *literary* activity (whereas, in the little pocket notebook, it's not like that, through the lack, specifically, of any order; not that what I note down, here and there, does not already have *form*; but the little pocket notebook is open to anything and everything.

[. . .]

Above, I especially wanted to point out that the association or the comparison is not of an *intellectual*, but of an *affective* nature. I think that this is the crux of the matter (by all means, to state it simply); the *emotion experienced* before it gives rise (if this is the case) to an explanation. Thereafter, all the *multifarious* involuntary playing with references on the level of—strong—childhood impressions, which escapes us and fulfills us, is given full rein, such that it is not, in effect, the clouds themselves that I am aiming at—in fact, it's them—but I will not reach them, will have no chance of reaching them (reach is not the word) unless, precisely, it is by means of a detour.

[. . .]

As I was going to set myself up in my observation post to "write about them," they disappeared.

Blue sky, cloudless. ("I am redone.")

Between them (I was going to write tween'em!), a *syntax*

— stormy syntax
syntax (of the) impossible

because, when two "terms" meet, there is a *shock*, bursting

STORMY SYNTAX ←

→ SYNTACTIC STORM

indeed, insist on that.

Written down in July (at Vernamiège)
mountains like clouds:
the more one looks at the mountains (even without haze), the more they change.

It's not just the sky or water that changes.

3 p.m.
Now streaks, sudden
stretch marks,
marked out in squares, for a moment (like waffles or "flakey" apple chips).

(but the urge, the urge to write is no longer there).

I digest—I am *heavy*—(as one says that a sky is *heavy*); I have a *heavily* coated tongue (a sky *heavy* with clouds); moreover, a tongue heavily coated is *white* (mine, this afternoon, figuratively)

but the (spoken) tongue, if it is white, would be the opposite of heavily coated.

white, and the thin layer (the "cloud layer") is crackled.

The mind is also heavy.

But clouds also travel. They are also the opposite of heavily burdened . . . vaporous. . .

Clouds
      —and on the lake, grouped into a regatta, sails. . .

Knowing how, in order to *break away*, to come back to this notebook only occasionally, without being riveted to it (as I have been since yesterday).

[. . .]

Becomes lighter, cracks open; increases in height

[a table. a notebook, a table of clouds]

dazzled, I can no longer look

whiteness (now almost) invisible

Like sounds (unperceived) and brief or lasting, calling out to each other, coming near each other, moving away, distant from each other within a great margin of silence, invisible whiteness

***

like sounds (unperceived)

near far from each other
blending, lasting or, brief, calling out to each other within a great margin of silence, from a distance

blending, lasting or, brief, calling out to each other, from a distance, within a great margin of silence

invisible whiteness

***

like sounds (unperceived)
blending, lasting or, brief, calling out to each other from a distance, in an expanse, a margin of silence

And the (false?) marble ceiling fixture in my parents' bedroom—very much a bearded Abraham, very much a figure emerging from a cloud—have I noted this down?—to whom I perhaps now owe my work on this notebook of clouds. . .

August 21

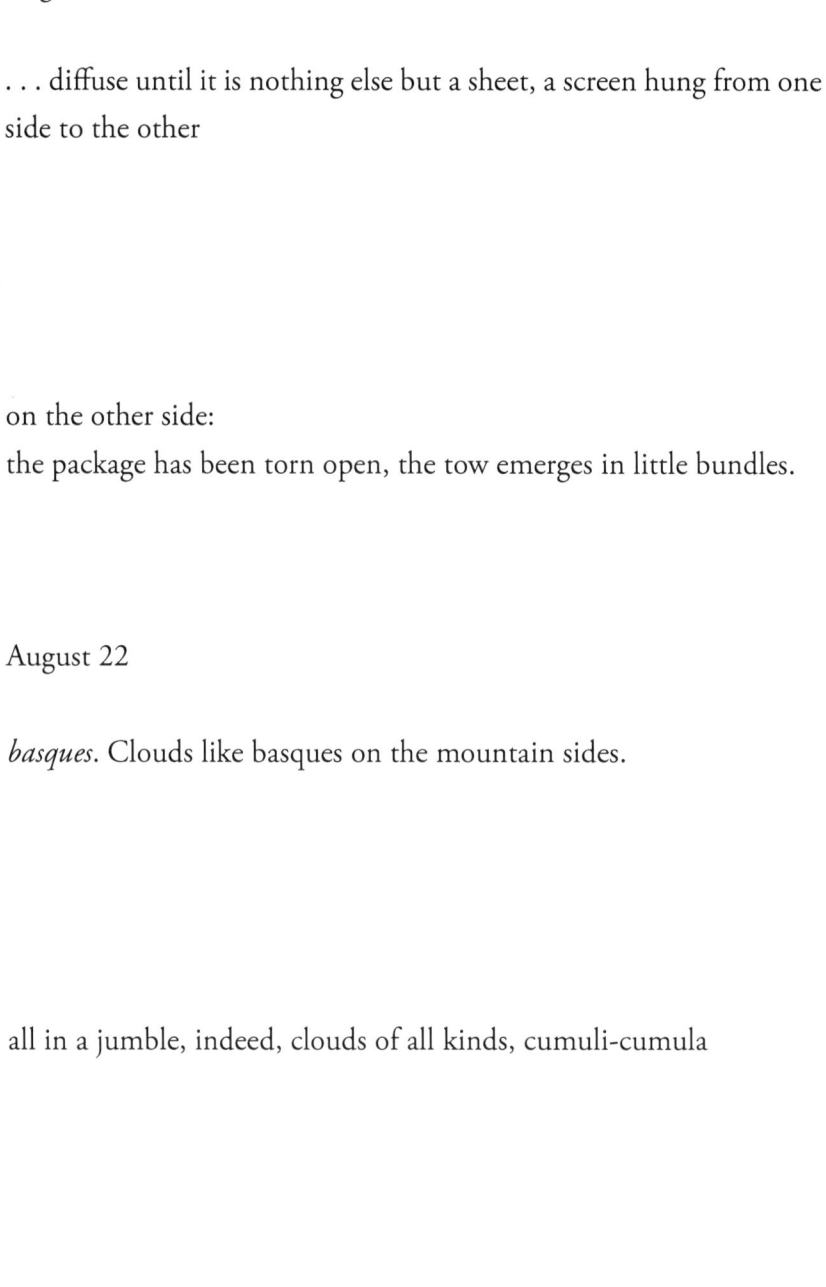

... diffuse until it is nothing else but a sheet, a screen hung from one side to the other

on the other side:
the package has been torn open, the tow emerges in little bundles.

August 22

basques. Clouds like basques on the mountain sides.

all in a jumble, indeed, clouds of all kinds, cumuli-cumula

A *Notebook of Clouds* would presuppose a more or less incoherent sequence, a *jumble* of notes, spontaneous jottings: but some pieces have taken form. This would presuppose the gathering—or comparing—of the two kinds of writing, but not as did Francis Ponge or Philippe Jaccottet. It would presuppose—this is where the difficulty lies—both remaining close to the spontaneous jottings and cheating, naturally, in any case sorting out and giving them a somewhat better form. I would willingly see the confrontation of the two kinds of writing—*verse*, *prose*, because I can't resolve the matter— similarities and divergences, parallels, as they overtake each other, "pursue" each other (in one way or another, the page layout should make both evident and admissible such an opposition, for example, by reserving the left-hand pages and italics for notes, and the right-hand pages and roman letters for "poems.").

[. . .]
From last spring, the rough draft retrieved:
Unmoving stormy furor, pinkish

with numerous new ones arriving
billowing, amassing, chubby-cheeked
(Zephyr, indeed, with his bloated cheeks)

Roses, white carnations, withering

Indeed, I can't manage to *hold my tongue*
(no more than my subject matter,
ever—a genuine piece of chewing gum—transforming itself)

Clouds, cloudlets, halos
stratus, nimbus, cumulus (scholarly pig Latin)

Martial de Brives: *Distilled exhalations*
(apropos of rain)

23 August

Satire (in the Latin sense, *Satura*, mixture. . .)

"Stuck between two clouds"

[. . .]

18 August (1984)

Today the sky is cloudless (without impurities), a transparency in which fade away in the distance (from my window) water, shore, sails (fortunately rare). A kind of whiteness instead of the azure, already autumnal...

Apropos of azure, Jean Tortel (*Interview* with Suzanne Nash): "The azure is precisely a sky of which one fears nothing. A beautiful, calm, blue, clear sky (. . .). A sky unlike one when a storm and rain are coming. A definite blue."
Clear (clearness transparency): one sees (one believes one sees) through. Clearness until it becomes whiteness. A bell, a dome that would rest over a void, a blue-tinted glass dome that would rest on the void.

Yes, already autumn.

August 18

Painted skies. In painting, skies are rarely blue, simply blue. Clouds filter the light; the sky is often a mixture, with the clouds adding up and laid out in tiers.

Gisèle's beautifully successful last wash drawings in which *slightly accumulate* (but also like pebbles forming a riverbed) little multicolored round clouds (also, a little, like scoops of different flavors of ice cream)—these, from the work that François has shown.

But since clouds are at stake, I'd have too many examples, wouldn't I? And because it's only fair that no cloud stands out—painting having merely rejuvenated, refreshed our eyes, having had no other function than that of *opening* our eyes (and not of imprisoning the gaze in a view, framing it), specifically that of conditioning of course (and in that, of enclosing, limiting) our gaze, but without constraining it, of encouraging it, on the contrary, within a given field (but everything is like this, everything is limitation), to *re-create*, just as well, if *nature imitates art*, can't it (or we) only produce incessantly again. Incessantly yielding to new suggestions, incessantly being not in front of the finished painting (and made by another person), but in front of the painting that will be made, that is possible, in the future, already vanished...

A NOTEBOOK OF RIDGES

A NOTEBOOK OF RIDGES

for Pierre Chappuis,
because a cloud sometimes looks like a ridge

How many times in your life? Every day? On each side a long slope downward.

A single trail along the ridge. Rarely an alternative once you are running the risk.

At best, a temporary sidestep because of a stone, a mound of dirt, a clump of grass.

Insignificant veerings.

What you know; then the ridge: the possible, the probable, or the impossible.

Even an avenue can be a ridge.

Because you've decided to take it, instead.

Let there be no mistake about it: The ridges were also with you, within you, in the flatlands. Here in the mountains they loom within and without.

Actually, in the flatlands, they also loomed without.

You weren't always aware of them.

Or you ignored them.

Is some sense of achievement or fulfillment possible without having taken risks, without having ventured out on ridges? Perhaps an uneasy sense—of whatever it is—but nonetheless the certainty that this sense is yours and yours alone.

Look and imagine
when you near the ridge. Look.
Look.

Dare.

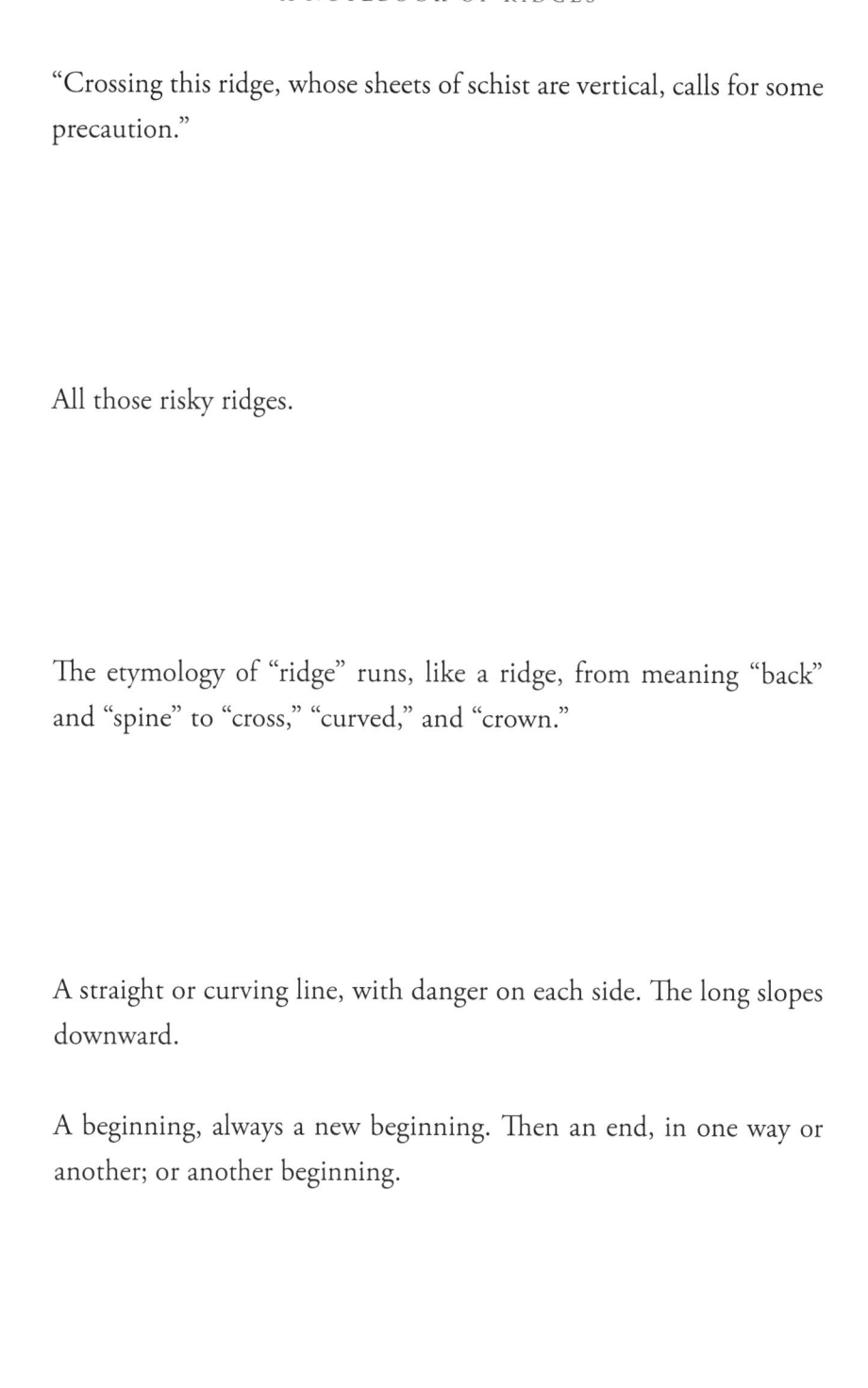

"Crossing this ridge, whose sheets of schist are vertical, calls for some precaution."

All those risky ridges.

The etymology of "ridge" runs, like a ridge, from meaning "back" and "spine" to "cross," "curved," and "crown."

A straight or curving line, with danger on each side. The long slopes downward.

A beginning, always a new beginning. Then an end, in one way or another; or another beginning.

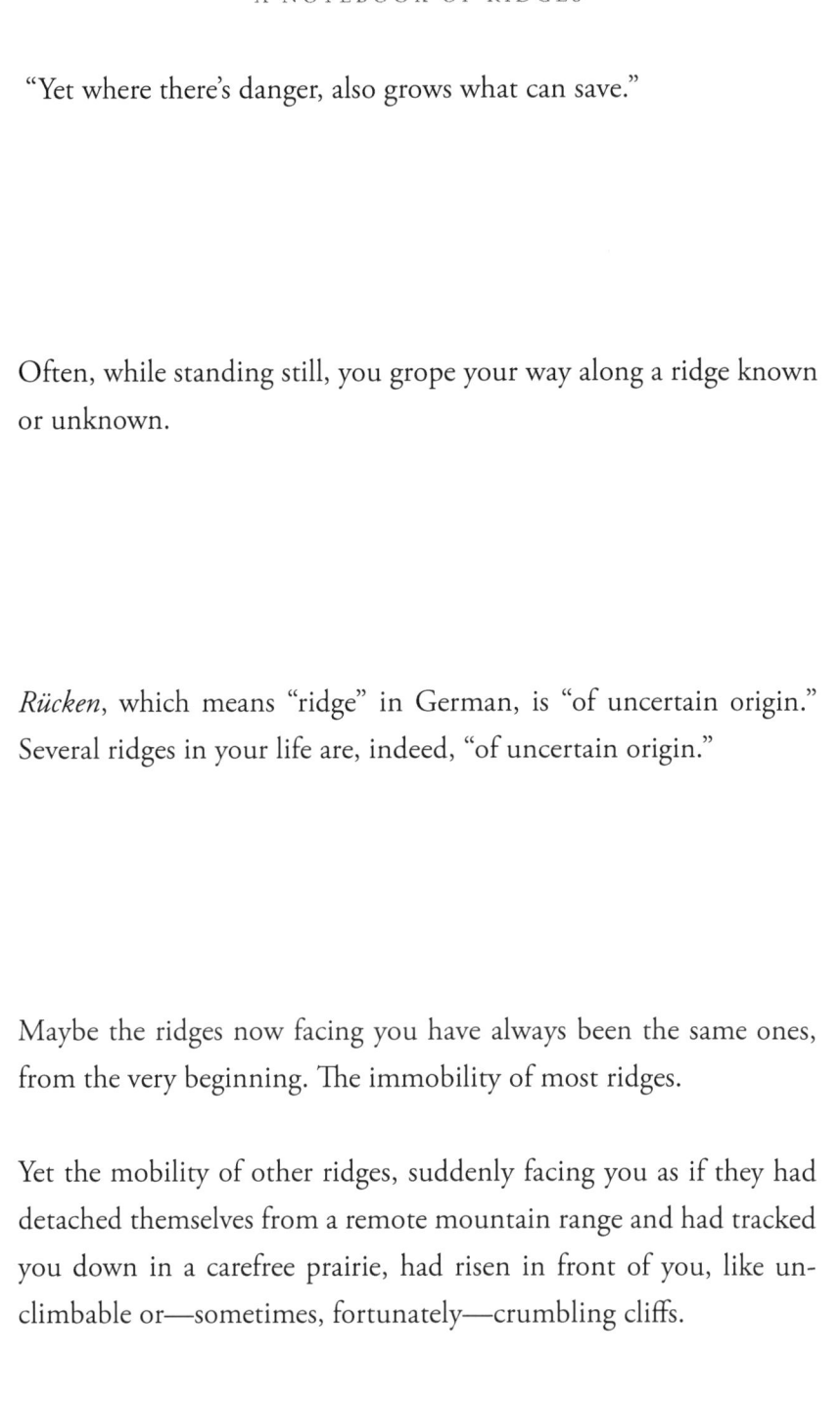

"Yet where there's danger, also grows what can save."

Often, while standing still, you grope your way along a ridge known or unknown.

Rücken, which means "ridge" in German, is "of uncertain origin." Several ridges in your life are, indeed, "of uncertain origin."

Maybe the ridges now facing you have always been the same ones, from the very beginning. The immobility of most ridges.

Yet the mobility of other ridges, suddenly facing you as if they had detached themselves from a remote mountain range and had tracked you down in a carefree prairie, had risen in front of you, like unclimbable or—sometimes, fortunately—crumbling cliffs.

Memories of ridges that others walked along. Their stories.

More of those memories than your own memories.

Actually, you have ventured out on few ridges.

Gazing from the overlook into the middle of the distant mountain range, you imagine shadows cast down from clouds—the sky is clear—onto ridges that you cannot see, will never see.

The horizon is one ridge facing you in every instant, as can be—once you become aware of its potentiality—every next step.

The horizon of every next step.

Your story, then their story:

A morning in Wyoming. An easy trail curving around a mountain for a few miles. The last hike taken with your father. At the end, in the parking lot as you are both readying to get into the car, two mountain climbers—burdened with ropes, harnesses, helmets, ice axes, belays, quickdraws, crampons, and carabiners—pass by, point at the ridge high above the trail and let you both know: "We're going to do that ridge."

You've stopped on cliff edges and overlooks much more often than you've walked along ridges.

This narrow ridge is pure stone.
When you bend down to retie the laces of your hiking boots, you touch the backbone of the earth, its vertebrae.

No.

You touch dust and hard stone.

Then you look off into space. Into air. Into emptiness.

Into yourself.

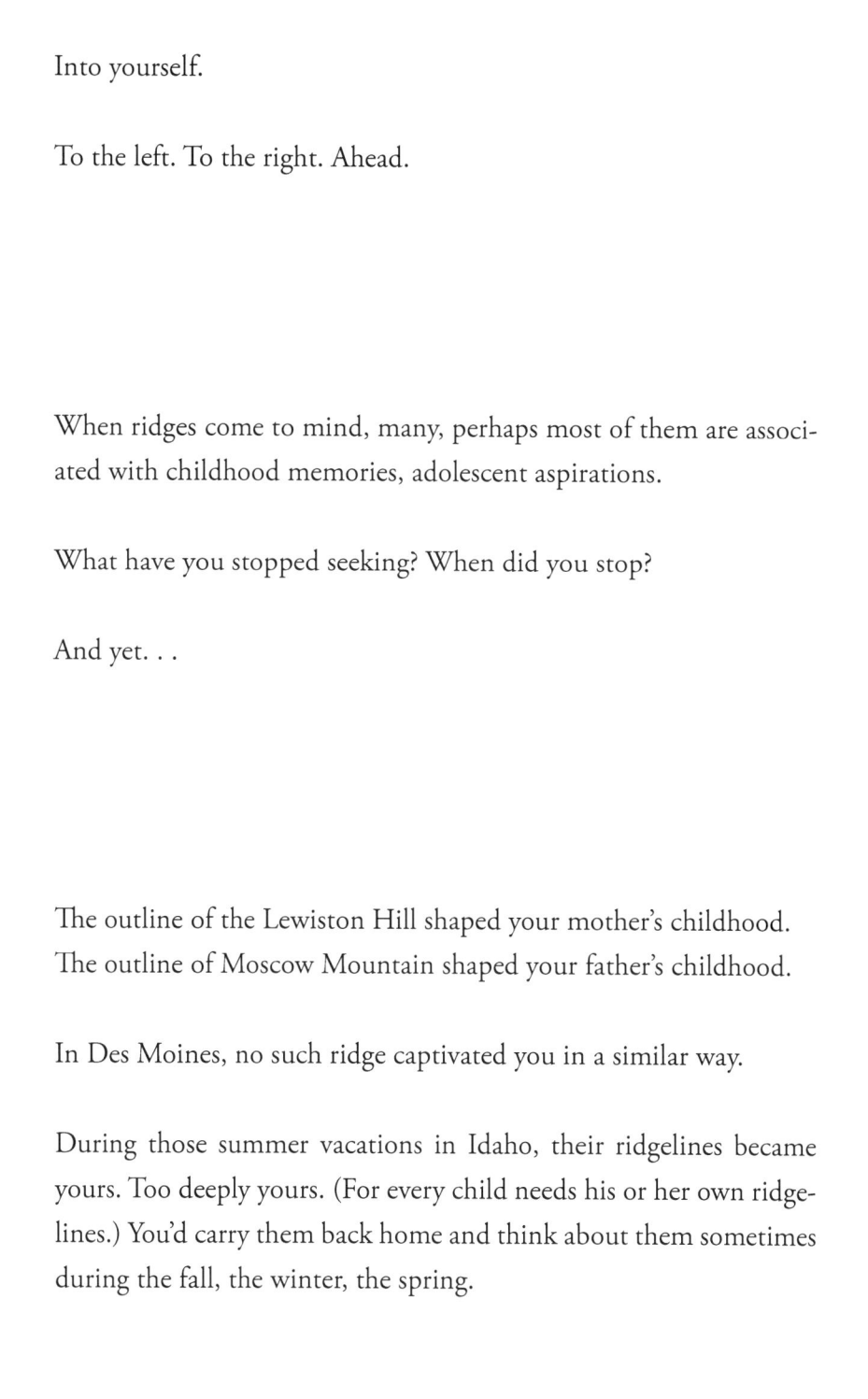

To the left. To the right. Ahead.

When ridges come to mind, many, perhaps most of them are associated with childhood memories, adolescent aspirations.

What have you stopped seeking? When did you stop?

And yet...

The outline of the Lewiston Hill shaped your mother's childhood. The outline of Moscow Mountain shaped your father's childhood.

In Des Moines, no such ridge captivated you in a similar way.

During those summer vacations in Idaho, their ridgelines became yours. Too deeply yours. (For every child needs his or her own ridgelines.) You'd carry them back home and think about them sometimes during the fall, the winter, the spring.

From your vantage point in the front seat of the Oldsmobile, as your father was driving up the Lewiston Hill to Moscow, the ridgeline at the top of the Hill would unfold into the plateau there, eventually into the curving contours of the Palouse Country, disappearing as if it had never existed. This always provoked your wonder, then a disappointment you kept to yourself.

But the ridgeline would be there, once again, after you had returned to Lewiston and, once again, gazed back up at the Lewiston Hill.

Actually, in your neighborhood in Des Moines, there was a kind of ridgeline: the exact (imaginary) line in the tar after which 48th Street descended to Urbandale Avenue: you were very small and for several years lived, as it were, on the ridge.

A childhood on the ridge and at lawn level.

Writing about ridges in places that have no apparent ridges, at least no mountain ridges. . .

You're in Angers.
You're in Nantes.
You're on the train to Paris.

Writing will bring you closer, you think, whereas you are inevitably given, at least at first, distance.

Imagine this distance as the twenty or so inches from one stone of the ridge to the next stone on which your next footstep must fall. So much depends on that footstep.

Raise your foot to take that step. . . and even if you take it, and then another one, and even if you reach the end of the ridge. . .

Ideally, writing takes the writer each time out onto a ridge.

But what ridge or ridges, in the final reckoning?

This is the question that must be asked of every line, every sentence.

Reckon with the ridge.

Take risks.
Take heed.

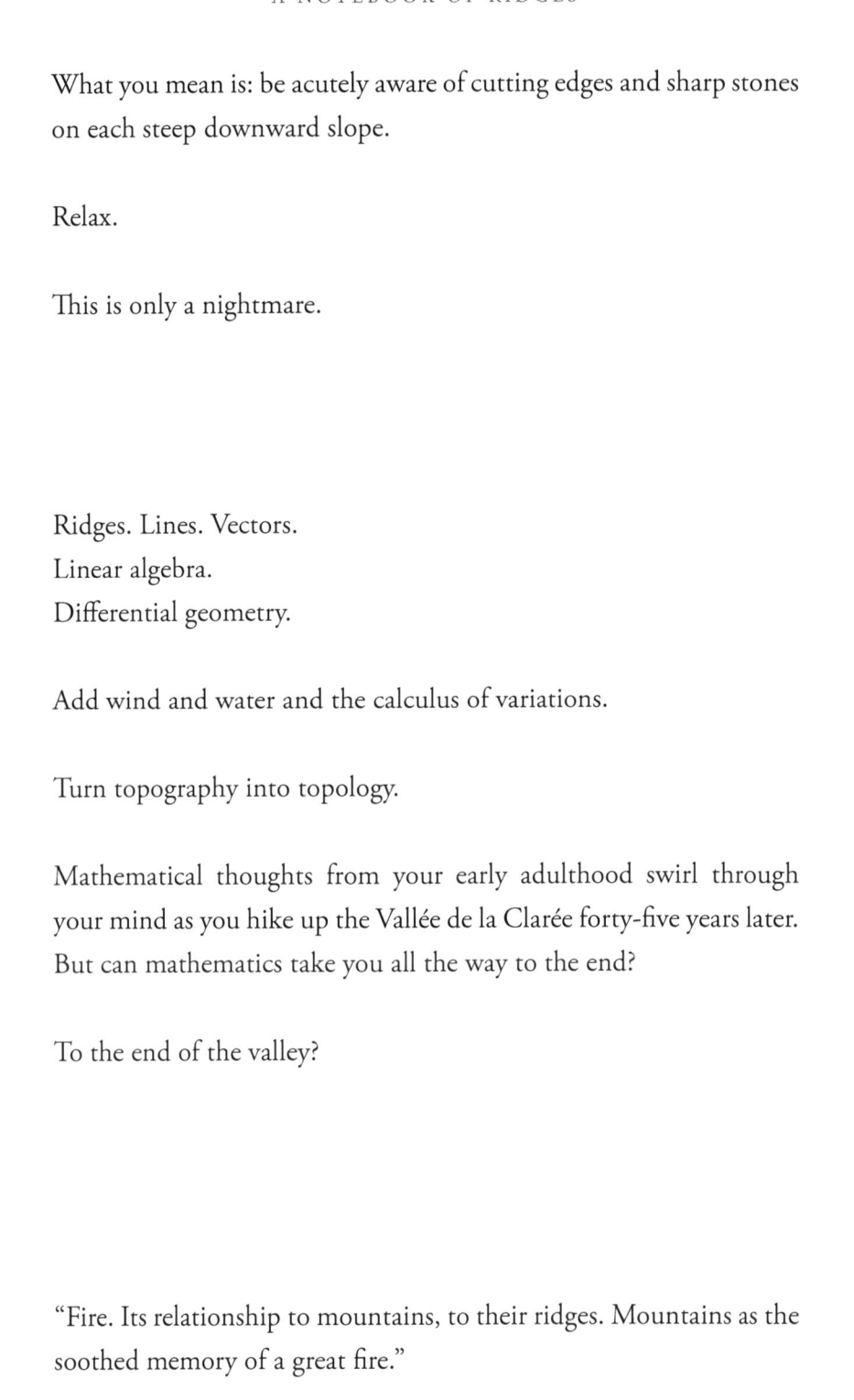

What you mean is: be acutely aware of cutting edges and sharp stones on each steep downward slope.

Relax.

This is only a nightmare.

Ridges. Lines. Vectors.
Linear algebra.
Differential geometry.

Add wind and water and the calculus of variations.

Turn topography into topology.

Mathematical thoughts from your early adulthood swirl through your mind as you hike up the Vallée de la Clarée forty-five years later. But can mathematics take you all the way to the end?

To the end of the valley?

"Fire. Its relationship to mountains, to their ridges. Mountains as the soothed memory of a great fire."

This wind must somehow have a ridge, somewhere.

Lac Cristol. Cristol Lake. However, "cristol" doesn't mean "crystal," but rather "windy ridge." On the old maps, it was spelled "Cristaoul" or "Cristavoul." From the Occitan word *cresta* ("ridge") and *oura* ("wind").

You also like the rocky and windy sound of the Italian word *cresta*, and that other Italian word, *crinale*, linked in your ear at least to the French word *crinière* "mane". The lion's mane.

Whenever you see the Atlantic once again, your eyes inevitably seek out the ridges—the crests, *les crêtes*—of the waves.

Pierre Chappuis writes of an "undulating ridge":

"Beeches, perhaps sorbs
giving meter
to the undulating ridge. . ."

You imagine a rippling ridge.

Undulating or rippling, at least some ridges are continuous, in front of you, behind you. Gentle, seemingly. Not ripped to shreds. Not sawtooth ridges.

You daydream of a gentle ridge formed by the tops of rolling forested hills. The crest of one of those hills. Its soothing silhouette at dusk. Dales, vales. . .

But now you must return to harsher ridges.

Words for ridge and ridgeline in your fifth language: κορυφή, κορυφογραμμή, ράχη. . .
The ridges, which you never crossed, during your months on the island of Samos.

The ridges that you crossed and, once you reached the other side, could no longer be crossed again in the other direction. No backtracking.

Another expression, το φρύδι του βουνού, literally means "the eyebrow of the mountain." But it was you, not the ridge, who watched yourself, on the ridge.

From your earliest memories, aspirations to the vertical as opposed to the horizontal. That the horizontal be re-established at the highest level possible. That the horizontal form a ridge.

Divagation:

Being on the ridge "of" nothingness.

Perhaps being "above" or "below" nothingness, as if there were a dividing line? As if the dividing line were a ridge?

The only perceptible entity?

Between being and non-being?

Between two slopes? And if so, what kind of slopes?

Not-Nothing would be Something, logically.

Why is there Something instead of Nothing?

Why is there Being instead of Non-Being?

Why is there a Ridge there, here, over there?

Another *divagation*:

Inverted ridge that would not be a V-shaped valley, not be a gorge, not be a ravine.

That would turn itself upside-down, then vanish. Freeing you at least from that ridge.

La clef des champs. La clef des crêtes. Setting off over the fields, over the ridges! Getting away from it all! But where is the key?

Three real ridges often come to mind and affect your fantasy:

the Col de la Rocheure—twice straddled.

beyond Saint-Véran, the Col de la Noire—once straddled.

the Black Glacier (Pré de Madame Carle), which you only contemplated from the beginning of the trail and studied in a hiker's guidebook: "Although it is only of moderate difficulty, this hike is not recommended to people prone to dizziness. The trail following the ridge is partly exposed and the empty space above the glacier can be felt. When it is snowing or raining, the trail can become dangerous."

Can the continental divide, up along that ridge, nonetheless somehow unify?

"Narrow footpaths recall that one side of the mountain never stops communicating with the other; that cries can beckon beyond that sharp blade-like ridge, that long jagged piece of flint, that enigma."

Three rivers have been ridges for you.

Some ridges have been implicit and left unmentioned, even left unthought of for long stretches of your lifetime.

(Such as a few ridges you have refrained from citing here.)

When you look back at a ridge, having crossed it. . .

When you imagine looking back at a ridge that you would have crossed if you had been able to do so. . .

The steep path and the choice, made at a crossroads in the larch forest, which brings you unknowingly within sight of a ridge.

Despite all kinds of maps at your disposition, some ridges are unforeseen, unforetold.

And even if you chose all your ridges. . .

Still another *divagation* or, rather, thought experiment:

The ridge of a thought.

    . . . of an intuition.

. . . of a feeling.

    . . . of a sensation.

(And so on.)

The ridges of bodies.

There are days when all available paths are ridges, in one way or another. Even sidewalks and pedestrian streets.

Ridge. Edge. Ridge. Ledge. (Grating half-rhymes.)

An almost impossible word to rhyme.

But remember: bridge.
The ridge as a bridge.

From here to here. From now to now.

Whatever emerges; is squeezed between two opposite forces; rises into prominence; is whetted into a narrow top along which runs a treacherous trail.

A fourth *divagation*:
I am / ridge \ I am not.
I am not / ridge \ I am not.

However covered with clouds, and whatever the clouds, the ridge remains.

Or under a clear sky.

Ridge for all seasons.

One question is: Will you have aspired to climb peaks or simply to grope your way along ridges, indifferent to, or apprehensive of, the summit? Often a mere mound!

Another question: Will you have mostly remained on the safe side, at the beginning of ridges?

A fifth *divagation*:
The ridge is not only *in* reality,
the ridge is reality.

Reality is a ridge.

Or, geometry notwithstanding, is a ridge the center, the essence of any given moment of reality?

The Crête du Diable. The jagged ridge, *la crête déchiquetée.*

Or a corroded crown from which all the rubies and emeralds have fallen away and which still weighs down on the head of a king.

The head of King Lear, having lost his first royal crown and now

"Crowned with rank fumiter and furrow weeds,
With hardocks, hemlock, nettles, cuckoo flow'rs,
Darnel, and all the idle weeds that grow
In our sustaining corn."

Here in the Vallée de la Clarée, more exactly: a crown of gypsum and rotting *cargneule*.

When the ridge fades into the night
itself becomes night

almost

it remains

a ridge

ever separates
day from day

Illusions and mirages:

Sometimes the shadows cast by clouds fall on a mountain slope in such a way that one ridge suddenly becomes apparent as two distinct successive ridges, sometimes rising at quite some distance from each another. And this is what is. There are truly two ridges.

From one vantage point, the remote ridge seems to rise or descend; from another, it seems to remain more or less level.

The ridge seemingly moves in one direction as the clouds above it are definitely moving in another direction yet seem to be motionless. As when you are sitting in a train and the train at the next platform starts to leave yet appears to remain at a standstill while you sense that it is you who are moving away.

Pierre Chappuis in his *Notebook of Clouds*:
"Extending from a gap ripped open from below in the thick layer massed over the land, and with their teeth turned upwards, a ridge bristling with spruce trees."

Sometimes you see peaks where there are ridges. Or you see ridges where there are peaks. Or you see neither and both are there. Or neither is there and you see both. Or only one of them.

ひらひらと　挙ぐる扇や　雲の峰
hira hira to / aguru ōgi ya / kumo no mine

"A fluttering fan / in the actor's rising hand / the ridge of a cloud."

As you stand at the Col de l'Izoard, you watch shadows of clouds moving across the scree wall of the Arpelin, seemingly caressing it. There is wind, then an absence of wind. That is, the whooshing—wooing, you would like to say: the alluring sound—of the south wind as it blows up the valley; a warm breeze; then the end of all sound. Yellowish, reddish, brownish hues appear, fade away on the scree. The whole scree wall seems to quiver, then dims, quiets down. Synaesthesia.

Through your binoculars, you notice a father and his son ascending the perilous ridge of the Arpelin.

The boy seems quite small.

Among your earliest ridges, *The Little Engine That Could*. The little locomotive climbing the steadily rising slope.

You remember the "Little Engine That Could" sweater that your grandmother knitted for you.

Or is it a photo that you remember? You were four years old and very ill.

The dark ridge against the sunlight.
The dark ridge against the night.

The sentiment that you are always gazing contre-jour.
The sentiment that you are always gazing contre-nuit.

As if daytime and nighttime remained at the farthest remove possible from you, had abandoned you to the reality in front of you.

And that whether this reality was in the light, or in darkness, no longer mattered.

A NOTEBOOK OF RIDGES

You can't see the mountain for the ridges.

La crête se détache toujours. The ridge always stands out and is "detached." Shouldn't you at last be learning how to "re-attach" the ridge to the whole mountain?

Even when black clouds descend across the ridgeline, the ridge remains, stands out at least in your immediate memory. You search for it, hope not to lose it.

Or hope to lose it.

Now it's dark and you must let the entire night pass—take place; take the place of everything else—before resuming your observations.

Sometimes, even often, the sunset beyond the ridge ultimately matters little.

All these metaphors you need to undo. . .

"Crestfallen." A farfetched etymological interpretation would associate dejection with falling off a crest, a ridge. . .

"The demon of analogy."

In prosody, a "cretic" is a metrical foot consisting of three syllables: long, short, long. Call it "ridge meter."

What will nourish you but must be kept secret is already hidden at the beginning of the ridge. You are climbing toward it. Look for it under a root, a rock. Take it, then go forth.

A recurrent dream leaves you halfway along the ridge when you awake.

Dendritic ridges, stratigraphic ridges, oceanic spreading ridges, crater ridges, volcanic crater or caldera ridges, fault ridges, dune ridges, moraines, eskers, volcanic sub-glacial ridges, shutter ridges. . .

On 19 February 1855, Henry David Thoreau writes to Mrs. Elizabeth O. Smith: "As for the good time that is coming, let us not forget that there is a good time *going* too, and see that we dwell on that eternal ridge between the two which neither comes nor goes."

You think so much about walking along ridges.

However, consider also the indifference of ridges, whether you walk along them or not. Walking along a ridge is not always the essential matter.

Sometimes you crawl along a ridge without even taking advantage of the perspective. Like a sightless man groping over rocks or grass, hand by hand, knee by knee.

"On the ridge, among the blades of wild grass."

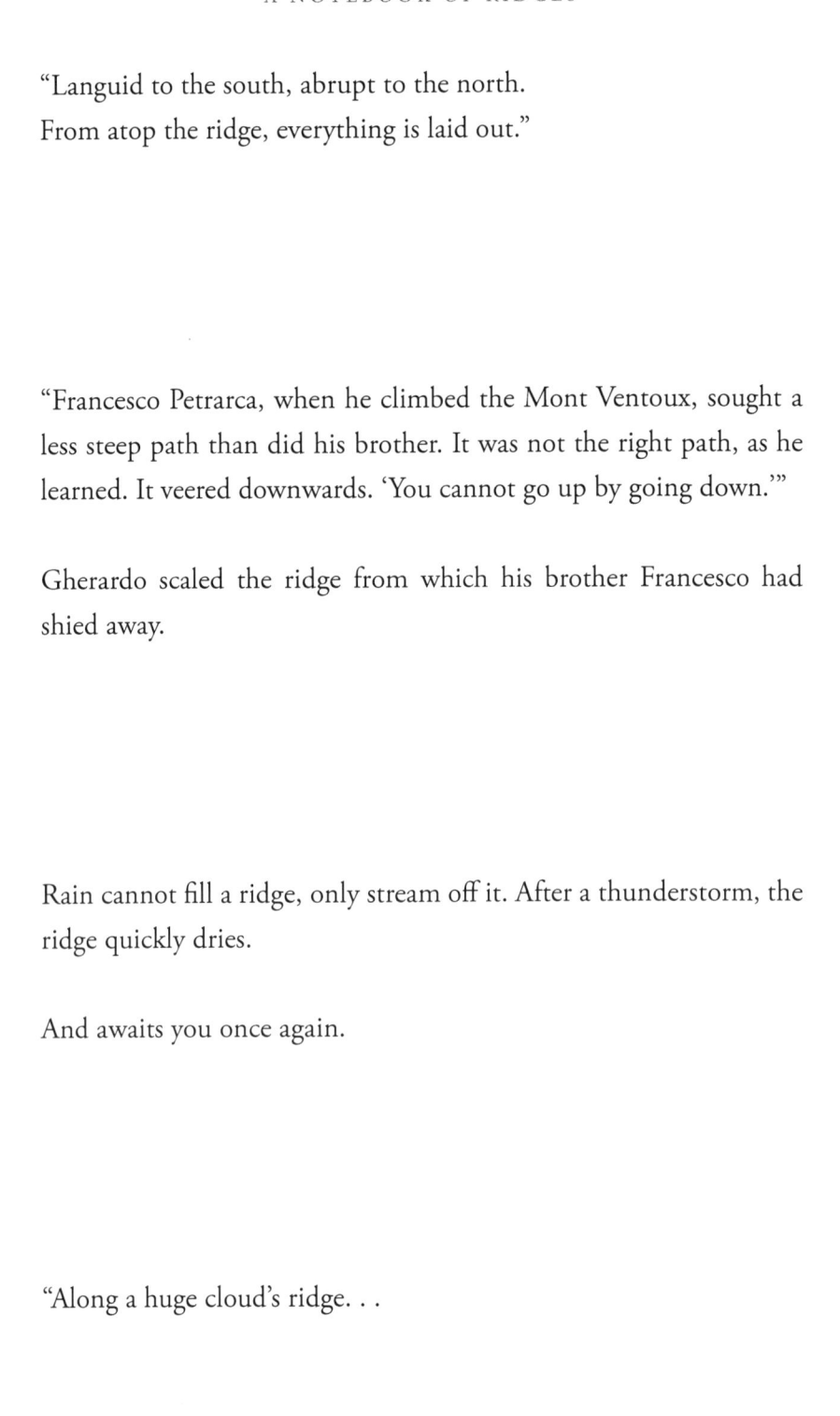

"Languid to the south, abrupt to the north.
From atop the ridge, everything is laid out."

"Francesco Petrarca, when he climbed the Mont Ventoux, sought a less steep path than did his brother. It was not the right path, as he learned. It veered downwards. 'You cannot go up by going down.'"

Gherardo scaled the ridge from which his brother Francesco had shied away.

Rain cannot fill a ridge, only stream off it. After a thunderstorm, the ridge quickly dries.

And awaits you once again.

"Along a huge cloud's ridge. . .

[. . .]

The visions all are fled—the car is fled
Into the light of heaven, and in their stead
A sense of real things comes doubly strong. . ."

"This mountain landscape in which, in the middle of a dark ridge, a peak rises as bright as a spear point cut out of a diamond: a supernatural light like those you see only in dreams; and it was a dream."

On the way up to the ridge, you suddenly wish to write about the larch forest—a nearly pure larch forest: no other kinds of trees—through which you are passing.

But no words come to mind but these.

Whatever the ridge, remember the name of the stream that cascades down from it and that you spot far below.

Remember the Arc
the Clarée

for the rest of your life.

Remember the Raccoon, even if the ridge running along it was merely a muddy bank beneath the oaks.

You were so small and that bank was so high

for the rest of your life.

Most ridges you only contemplate for a short while before you grasp your binoculars, which are hanging by a strap around your neck, and search for chamois on the slope below the ridge.

Sometimes your hands tremble when you look through your binoculars, which are heavy. When your hands don't tremble, the focus is very precise.

A steep slope and its ridge rise above you while so many rocks lie scattered in your midst. The rocks have probably avalanched down from the ridge rather recently, as is shown by the scarce vegetation that has grown up and over them.

You're not at all sure that beauty will still be at stake when you're on the ridge.

The ridge is on the horizon, but already it affects the here and now, and makes a new ridge deep inside you.

Redstarts flutter in the high grass. What do they know of ridges? Their ridges are beyond your capacity to know, to imagine.

(A redstart alights on the balcony within a few feet from where you are jotting this down. You'd like to take a picture of it. You reach for your camera. Already the redstart has flown away.)

When the clouds come down over all the ridges, fill the valley as if—but this is mere fear—forever. . .

Ridges in the background, ridges in the foreground.

Christ has been crucified on the hill overlooking the town. But as you watch him being gently brought down from the cross, in a 16th century fresco painting in the church of Plampinet, you cannot help but notice beyond the scene—through the scene, actually, to the right of the cross and below Christ's left leg—then beyond the towers and ramparts of the town, a vast field in the distance bordered, on the remote horizon, by a peak and a mountain range.

Then your eyes return to Christ, who remains frozen in his descent—this is a painting—, to John holding up a devastated swooning Mary, and to Mary Magdalene, whose sadness shows that she has known, from the very beginning, that all this would come to pass.

Sometimes the unreachable ridges are right in front of you.

A ridge that cannot be found on any map. And yet you spot it. Or at least admit to yourself that it is there.

"In order to get around several serrated formations on the ridge, we went down the northeastern slope to the right, through a corridor full of huge boulders, by which we arrived in a few moments at a bigger corridor on the same slope just at the place where it takes a frighteningly steep downward plunge."

Where there is a horizon, there is a ridge.
Where there is no horizon, there is a ridge.

Saint-Beuve forged the image of a "brilliant ridge of syllables" when he was analyzing Chateaubriand's style: "In his writing, beauty—even the beauty of his thinking—depends too much on form; it is as if it were chained to the peak of words [. . .], to the brilliant ridge of syllables."

Beware of any desire to shine when you're on the ridge.

"The pauses or blank spaces between fragments, maxims, or notes whose words form, to recall Yves Bonnefoy's phrase, 'the ridgeline of a silence'..."

Climbing up to ridges over ill-chosen steep itineraries for which, from the onset, there are few footholds, few handholds.

The disturbing inner drive to reach a ridge that can be like a disturbing spontaneous attraction to another body.

The lip of the ridge. Cupid's bow.

On the ridge, you will be dizzy.

When Horace-Bénédict de Saussure projected to climb the Mont Blanc, he prepared himself for dizziness by staring into abysses and rationalizing his fear.

If you know how to walk a straight line, you won't fall off to the left, to the right. This is what you keep telling yourself.

As you climb to the ridge, you notice that the Aiguille Noire—the Black Needle—sometimes vanishes behind a contour of the slope to your left, only to reappear and then, after a few such disappearances, to remain ever in front of you.

The forest climbs the slope, then is blocked by a wide strip of vertical naked stone, before trees once again appear, above the stone, and subsequently form a new, increasingly dense forest that covers the ridge. You focus your thoughts on being and barrenness, but this does not suffice.

Staring at the naked stone, you seek a deeper meaning (where there is surely none) for a similar kind of failure, infertility, in your own life.

But up there, it's a matter of stone and slope.

On the ridge of the Mount of Olives, David wept, and then Christ wept, over Jerusalem.

Yves Bonnefoy: "The interruption of the line in Cézanne's representation of the ridge [in his paintings of the Mont Sainte-Victoire], its brokenness, indicates—by its very absence—Presence."

Gazing at the Grande Chalanche, you wonder where you would leave out segments of the ridgeline. But as you ponder this question—how to segment the ridge—you are already gazing elsewhere, or nowhere at all; you are gazing at something inside you. And you are by no means an artist in the throes of painting, where your spontaneous manual decisions would also be based on experience, as well as on intuitions.

Gaze once again at the Grande Chalanche and think of nothing else.

Forget what you have written here.

Try to forget the ridge.

See it anew.

A sixth divagation:

Eliminate the ridgeline and try to open up the top of the mountain? . . . To what?

And the ridgeline is re-established.

The ridgeline is ever re-established.

The Crête du Diable, once again. Because of the near-vertical slant of the sunrays, King Lear's crown suddenly seems more distant, to fade into a billowing cumulus cloud.

It's no longer even a pathetic crown. It's a distant theater curtain that must ever remain closed, even when the cumulus has evaporated.

Light so bright on the wheat fields that the very fields become light and the remote ridge fades from the present moment, your present moment.

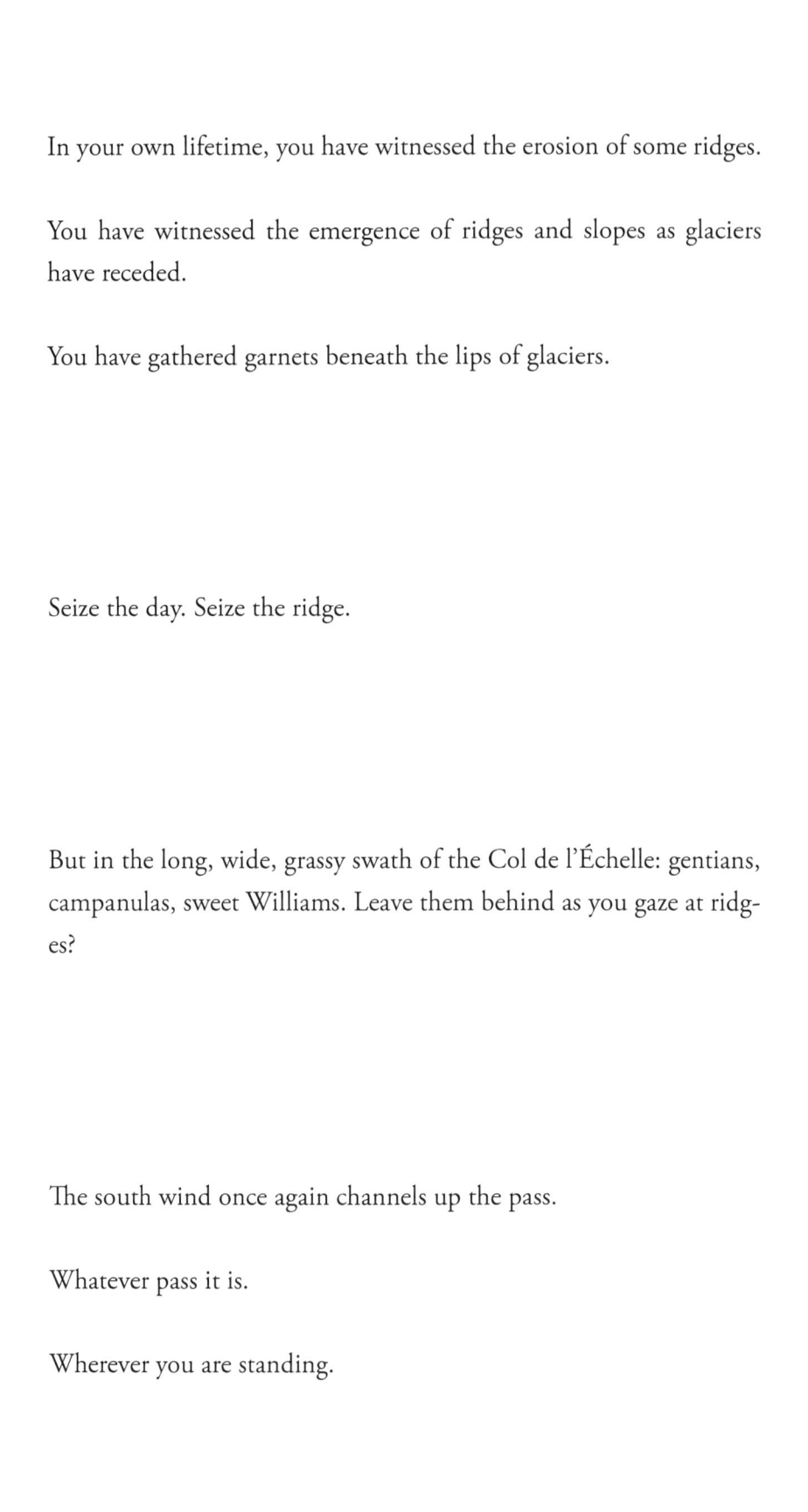

In your own lifetime, you have witnessed the erosion of some ridges.

You have witnessed the emergence of ridges and slopes as glaciers have receded.

You have gathered garnets beneath the lips of glaciers.

Seize the day. Seize the ridge.

But in the long, wide, grassy swath of the Col de l'Échelle: gentians, campanulas, sweet Williams. Leave them behind as you gaze at ridges?

The south wind once again channels up the pass.

Whatever pass it is.

Wherever you are standing.

And one day, at a given moment—the last moment given to you—all these ridges will dwindle to stars in the inaccessible sky, and then to points whose width is zero.

("A point is a dimensionless geometric object having no properties except location.")

Névache, 22 July – 5 August 2017
(and in a few other places before and since then)

The Word and the Stream

What is this word, this name?

It is the name of a stream.

La Clarée.

More than a stream of clear water. That which is clear. Clearness. Water which, in its flowing, bears forth clearness; which offers clearness. Which offers itself.

Clearness as it flows down, falls, from the ridge between banks of glacier-crumbled quartz, schist, *cargneule*.

Clearness then opening out as the water meanders through the marshy terraces that form the high valley.

Before the water falls again, over the rocks.

Ever again.

The water falls. And makes noise. A kind of music.

Ever again.

In early spellings, *clarée* was also written *claret*, *clairet*. Looking at the two words, listening to them, especially to *clairet*, you perceive the clearness as narrower, more precious perhaps, shallower.

You think of the wine called *clairet*. It is a dark rosé. Or a light red wine, a pale red wine.

In jewelry, *clairet* means a gem with a very pale color.

Look and listen in English. Then in French. Then in English once again.

Clearness. Clarity. Clarté. Clarée. Clearness.

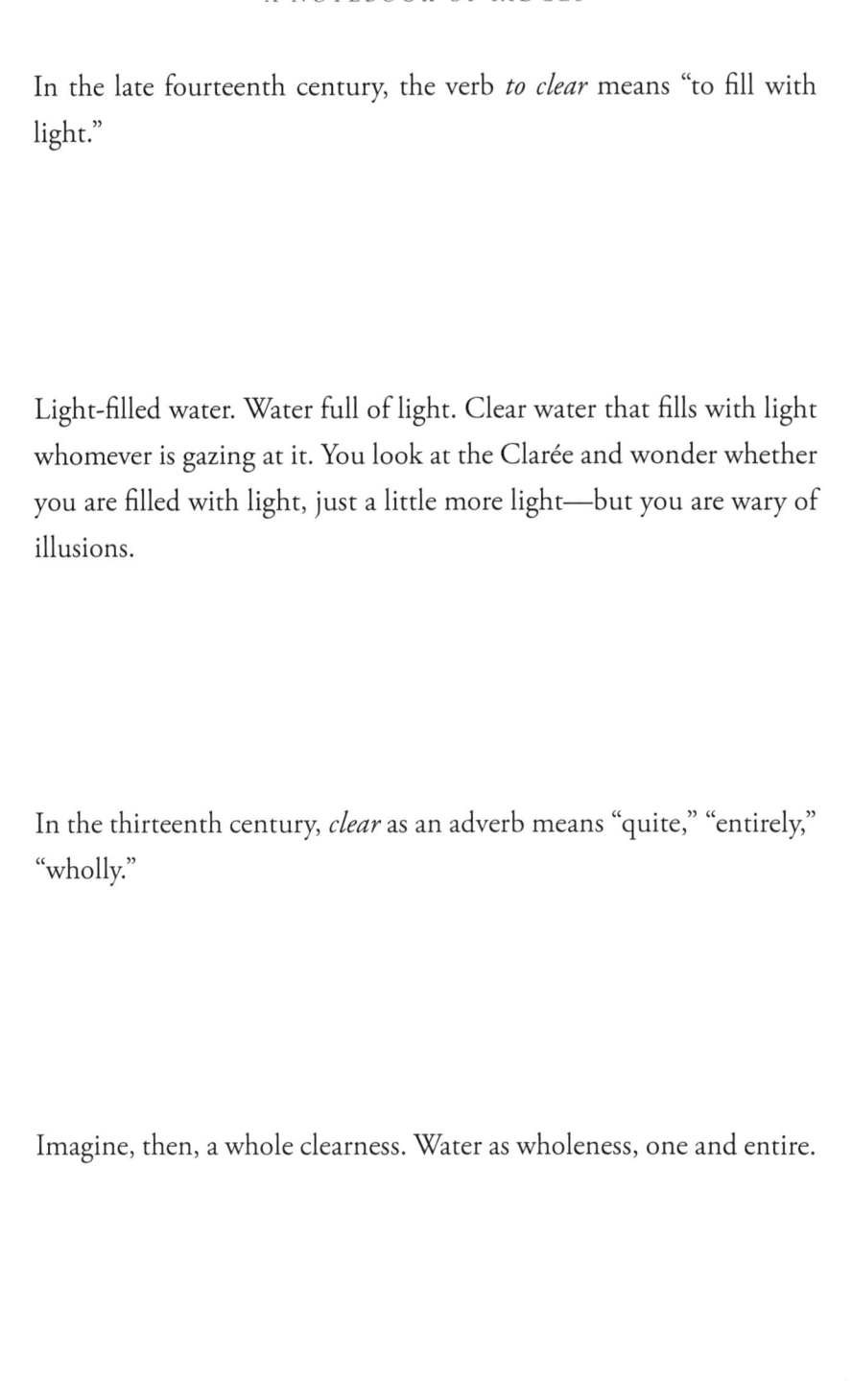

In the late fourteenth century, the verb *to clear* means "to fill with light."

Light-filled water. Water full of light. Clear water that fills with light whomever is gazing at it. You look at the Clarée and wonder whether you are filled with light, just a little more light—but you are wary of illusions.

In the thirteenth century, *clear* as an adverb means "quite," "entirely," "wholly."

Imagine, then, a whole clearness. Water as wholeness, one and entire.

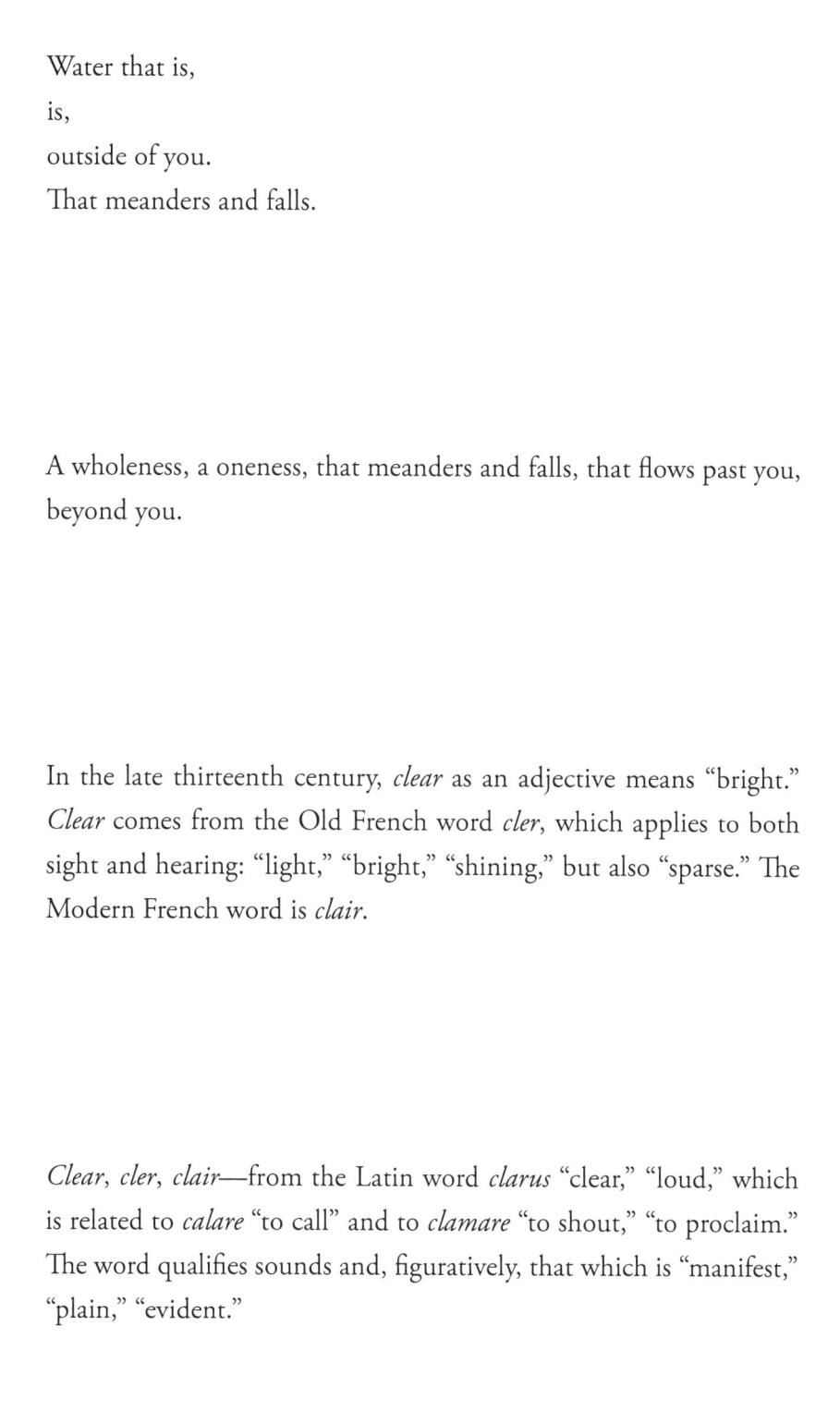

Water that is,
is,
outside of you.
That meanders and falls.

A wholeness, a oneness, that meanders and falls, that flows past you, beyond you.

In the late thirteenth century, *clear* as an adjective means "bright." *Clear* comes from the Old French word *cler*, which applies to both sight and hearing: "light," "bright," "shining," but also "sparse." The Modern French word is *clair*.

Clear, *cler*, *clair*—from the Latin word *clarus* "clear," "loud," which is related to *calare* "to call" and to *clamare* "to shout," "to proclaim." The word qualifies sounds and, figuratively, that which is "manifest," "plain," "evident."

Singing and shouting. Showing. A sonorous celebration of clearness as the Clarée flows past you.

Clear, therefore, as the spreading of sound and the spreading of light. Like the English adjective *loud*, when used of colors.

Listen to the Clarée when you are looking at it, look at the Clarée when you are listening to it.

Then simply look. Simply, listen. If you can look and listen without words, without the word.

But sometimes you look and listen better because of words.

Whole sounds. Pure sounds. Besides its visible clearness, the sonorous clearness of the Clarée as it babbles over the rocks.

Babble: sparkling water flowing and also sounds. Like those of a baby when it first discovers its ability to make sound and becomes aware that it is making sound. Imagine the purest sparkling, the purest, most joyful babbling. A soft babbling that is so whole that it is clear and, although soft, also loud.

Although loud, also soft.

A soft loudness. A dim brightness. Almost a shy brightness, which can be heard.

Facing the Clarée, you marvel at this as you would at a newborn child. Marvel because what is clear—manifest, plain, evident: a child as it comes into being—is unclear when you ponder it.

Being is clear; then unclear. Even as the Clarée is ultimately unclear to you.

"Ein Rätsel ist Reinentsprungenes," writes Hölderlin. "A riddle is that which surges up, springs up, emerges, comes to the surface, purely." A pure surging forth. A clear emergence. A riddle that is offered by the Rhine—to Hölderlin—and by the Clarée. The very fact, the very phenomenon, the very riddle of water: that of water flowing, of water nourishing roots and lives.

What roots? For instance, the roots of cotton grass in the high marshy meadows of the Vallée de la Clarée. The clusters of cotton grass appear to you as a riddle. Or a miracle.

What lives? The water flows through human lives, through the lives of wild animals that come down from the slopes by night, through herds of sheep and goats that graze nearby during the day.

A thirst-quenching clearness that you understand; then do not understand.

Your aliveness as a clearness—what is manifest, plain, evident—that you understand; then do not understand.

This very clearness—what you understand and do not understand—flows past you.

"La Clarée ne tarit jamais." "The Clarée never runs dry, is never without water." The man who speaks these words knows, has long known. He has never seen, never heard, the Clarée without water.

Clear water, but you sense more. Or wish for more? Suspend your wishing as long as you can. Peer into the real water.

But is this clear water that you see, real?

According to folk legend, the stream is itself—herself—the goddess and guardian of the water that begins in the lake just over the ridge, that rushes down to the lush awaiting meadows where it meanders. Then rushes again. Then meanders. Then rushes.

Her name is Clarée. Call her Clearness. She watches over herself, over movement, over slope, all the while being herself, and movement, and slope.

"La Mère de l'Eau," "The Mother of Water," as the stream was also once called locally.

You secretly beckon to the Mother of Water: "I am growing blind and deaf. Help me see all the shades of sound—help me hear all the tones of color—as the clearness flows past me."

Yet the Mother of Water is water. Yet the goddess of the Clarée is the Clarée. Clearness is clearness.

Are you beckoning to your own mother?

She is gone.

As a larch needle falls into the flowing water of the Clarée, floats by, has long floated by.

Yet you still hear her speaking to you when you were a child. And later. At the end. Brief flowings of words—coming toward you, passing by.

A few words spoken in a certain way form a clearness. The clearness flows by, but also remains for a while.

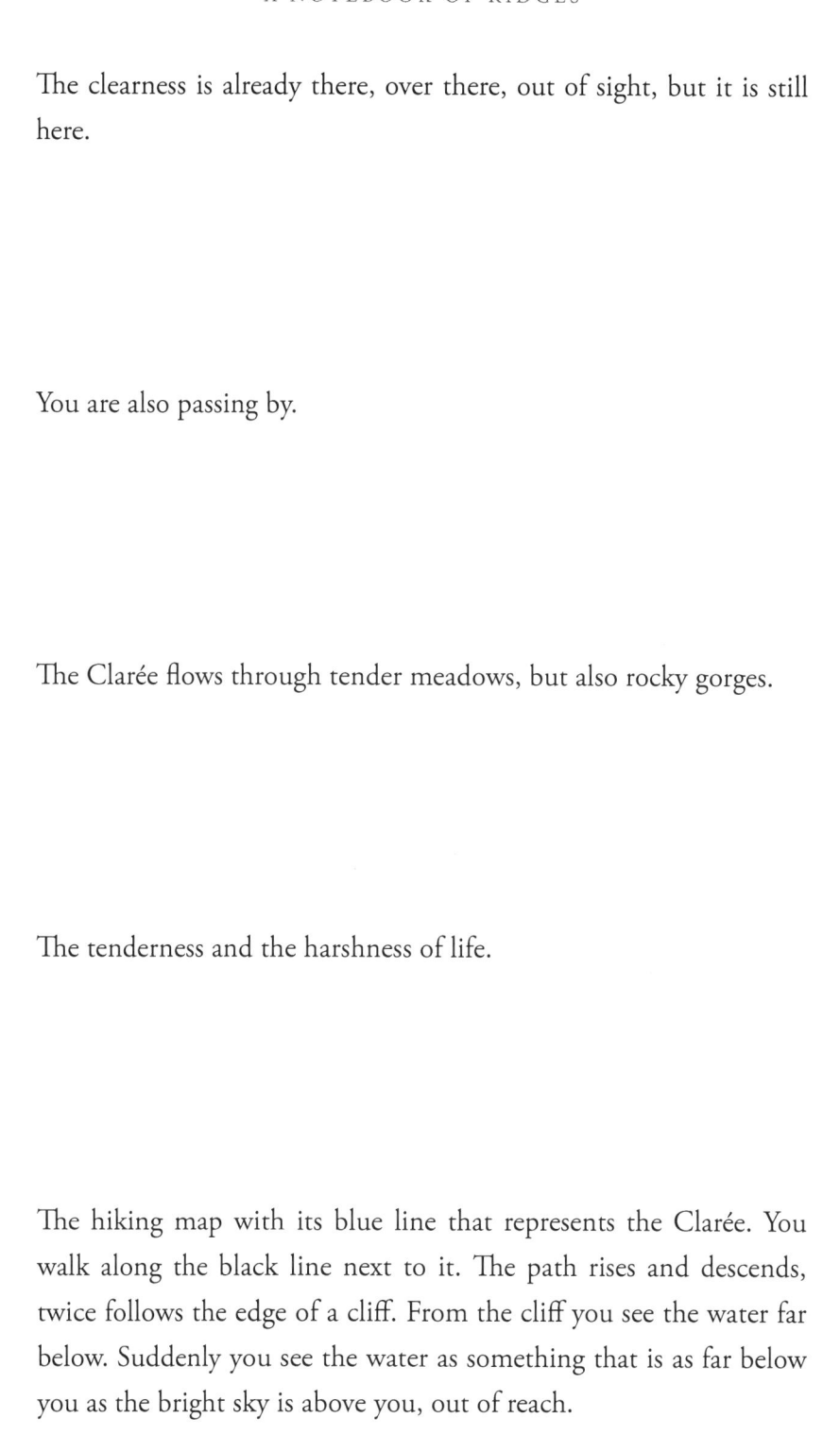

The clearness is already there, over there, out of sight, but it is still here.

You are also passing by.

The Clarée flows through tender meadows, but also rocky gorges.

The tenderness and the harshness of life.

The hiking map with its blue line that represents the Clarée. You walk along the black line next to it. The path rises and descends, twice follows the edge of a cliff. From the cliff you see the water far below. Suddenly you see the water as something that is as far below you as the bright sky is above you, out of reach.

In John Bunyan's *Pilgrim's Progress*, the Celestial City can be spotted from the Delectable Mountains, indeed from Mount Clear. You rename this mountain in French: Mont Claré.

You set down the book, which belonged to your mother. You hike down from the Delectable Mountains. Now you wish to look, not from afar, nor into any distance except that of the riddle of water.

You are nearing the riddle. If there is one.

You look at the Clarée. The riddle of clearness?

The nearest riddle, the most remote riddle?

Touch,
touch the clear water.

And listen.

NOTES

Notes to A Notebook of Clouds

Pierre Chappuis has blended quotations and literary allusions into several texts, as integral parts of his prose and poetry, that is, without using the quotations as "illustrations" of arguments, but rather as poetic images intimately participating in his own perceptions of clouds. I've noted the sources below, along with a few translation issues.

(p. 3) The epigraph ". . .land and cloud. . ." comes from *Sommerreise* (Summer Journey, 1903), by the Austrian writer Hugo von Hofmannsthal (1874-1929). Chappuis uses Albert Kohn's translation: "Voyage d'été," *Lettre à Lord Chandos et autres essais*, Gallimard, 1980, p. 93.

(p. 7) The text by the French novelist Stendhal (1783-1842) comes from his *Voyages en Italie* (Gallimard-Pléiade, p. 477), chapter "Rome, Naples et Florence (1826)," specifically the passage "Pietramala, 19 janvier 1817."

(p. 9) "*Clouds, cloudlets*." Chappuis opens his French text with three words: "nuages," "nuées," "nues." The words are synonyms, but with "nuances" between them. Note that these three words as well as "nuance" have the same derivation: from Latin *nubes* ("cloud"). For the translator, the problem is unsolvable: "nuages" as well as the poetic "nuées" and "nues"—whose levels of diction are thus more literary—are most often rendered by "clouds." A "nuée" tends to be perceived as "a cloud of big dimensions (vast or thick)," according to the dictionary *Le Robert*. A "nue" is a "cloud or an ensemble of clouds" (*Le Robert*). I've taken the liberty of using two words, "clouds and cloudlets" (necessarily a small cloud), to recall above all the differences in levels of diction.

(p. 9) "Stilled beneath the oppressive cloud." This is one of the most notoriously obscure poems written by Stéphane Mallarmé (1842-1898). E. H. and A.M. Blackmore, from whom I have borrowed this English version, translate the first two strophes of the sonnet as follows: "Stilled beneath the oppressive cloud / that basalt and lava base / likewise the echoes that have bowed / before a trumpet lacking grace // O what sepulchral wreck (the spray / knows, but it simply drivels there) / ultimate jetsam cast away / abolishes the mast stripped bare" (*Collected Poems and Other Verse*, Oxford Classics, 2006).

NOTES

(p. 9) "Her head on her arm and her arm on the cloudlet." La Fontaine (1621-1695), "Le Songe de Vaux" (1729).

(p. 9) "I love clouds. . . passing clouds. . ." Charles Baudelaire (1821-1867), "L'étranger" (The Outsider, The Stranger), *Petits poèmes en prose* (1869).

(p. 10) Urabe Kenko. Also called Yoshida Kenko (1283-1350). Japanese author and Buddhist monk. *Idle Hours* was published ca. 1330-1335.

(p. 10) Du Fu, the Chinese poet (712-770).

(p. 10) "blue dome of air." This line by the English poet Percy Blythe Shelley (1792-1822) is found in the last strophe of his poem "The Cloud": "I am the daughter of Earth and Water, / And the nursling of the Sky; / I pass through the pores of the ocean and shores; / I change, but I cannot die. / For after the rain when with never a stain / The pavilion of Heaven is bare, / And the winds and sunbeams with their convex gleams / Build up the blue dome of air, / I silently laugh at my own cenotaph, / And out of the caverns of rain, / Like a child from the womb, like a ghost from the tomb, / I arise and unbuild it again."

(p. 10) "The grandiose architecture of the clouds leaves me with my chaos." Pierre-Albert Jourdan (1924-1981), *L'Entrée dans le jardin* (1981). See *The Straw Sandals: Selected Poetry and Prose*, Chelsea Editions, 2011, p. 114.

(p. 11) "The room abandoned to the clouds. . . the clouds left to the sea. . ." Jacques Dupin (1927-2012), *Une apparence de soupirail* (1982).

(p. 11) "On the grass of the clouds a plowshare of light." Pierre Voélin (b. 1949), *La Nuit osseuse* (Castella, 1984) or *To Each Unfolding Leaf: Selected Poems 1976-2015* (Bitter Oleander Press, 2017, p. 40).

(p. 11) "The potholed alleyways of cloudy spells." In French, "Passages nuageux pleins de cahots" is a pun. The expression "passages nuageux" means "cloudy spells," but also cloudy "passages" in the sense of a lane, an alleyway, etc.

NOTES

(p. 13) "faire chou blanc." This French expression, literally "to do (behave like) a white cabbage," means "to draw a blank" or to go out in search of something and come back with nothing.

(p. 14) "Barre de nuages. . ." The French poem is based on several puns. "Barre," whose primary sense is "bar" or "rod," has other metaphorical extensions or associations when it is used with other words. "Barre de nuages" thus suggests a "wall" of thick clouds, in the distance, such as occurs when a cold or warm front arrives. "Barre d'appui" is, specifically, a "window rail," and more generally a "bar" on which one can "lean." "Barre au front" is a popular expression meaning "headache," literally to have "a bar on one's forehead"; but the French "front" also means "front" in the meteorological sense. "Barre fixe" is a "chinning bar" in gymnastics, but it can also be read here as a "stable bar," a "bar" that has been attached to something; arguably, a "wall" (bar) of clouds that remains in a fixed position." My translation is a free interpretation that maintains the repetition, not of "barre," but of "front."

(p. 19) "$C_h\ C_i$ (fib. int.)". This scientific formula refers to high clouds (C_h) that are, specifically of the "Ci (Cirrus) fib (fibratus) int (intortus)" type.

(p. 21) "cow tails" and "windy feet" are two Quebecois expressions. The former suggests long tapered clouds, whereas latter means sunrays breaking through clouds.

(p. 35) "Goethe's stupid advice to Caspar David Friedrich." The friendship between Johann Wolfgang von Goethe (1749-1832) and Caspar David Friedrich (1774-1840) waned in 1816 when the writer asked the artist to do some paintings of clouds for his meteorological studies. Friedrich, who did not consider himself to be a realist painter and who was interested in divine or metaphysical mysteries, was put aback by the request.

(p. 36) Émile Littré (1801-1881), the great French lexicographer, whose dictionary (first edition: 1863-1872) is still often used by French writers.

(p. 37) The German poet Nelly Sachs (1891-1970) uses the word *Traumsandufern* in her poem "Warum die schwarze Antwort des Hasses" ("Why the Black Answer of Hate"), which is found in her collection *Steinverdunklerung* (1949); see her collection *Fahrt ins Staublose* (Suhrkamp, 1988, p. 100). Chappuis is using the French edition *Brasier d'énigmes*, translated by Lionel Richard, Les Lettres Nouvelles, 1967, p.74.

(p. 41) "Pigeon vole" ("Pigeon flies"), which is somewhat similar to "Simon Says," is a children's game based on speed and comprehension. One of the children pronounces the name of an animal or object, followed by "flies: "Pigeon flies," "duck flies," chair flies," etc. If the animal or object actually flies, the other children raise their hands; if the animal of object does not fly, then the children need to keep their hands on the table. If a child makes a mistake, he is eliminated. With "nuages," Chappuis is suggesting that the child is raising his hand; with "table," that the child is keeping his hand on the table. "Simon Says" is a more physical game, which I'm trying to suggest by this free translation.

(p. 43) "If it's formless, he gives it as formless." From the so-called "Lettre du Voyant" ("Letter of the Seer") written by the French poet Arthur Rimbaud (1854-1891) to Paul Demeny on 15 May 1871.

(p. 46) "So that one face / is effaced by the stroke that the other face effaces". "Le Second Jour", by the writer and poet Guillaume Salluste Du Bartas (1544-1590).

(p. 49) Claude Debussy (1862-1918) composed his *Clouds* as one of his three *Nocturnes* (1897-1899), György Ligeti (1923-2006) his *Clocks and Clouds* (for orchestra and twelve female voices) in 1972-1973.

(p. 50) Chappuis compares the French artist Nicolas Poussin (1594-1665), who, by the way, is often evoked by contemporary French-language poets, to the Italian painters Francesco Guardi (1712-1793) and Giambattista Tiepolo (1696-1770).

(p. 51) The English painter William Turner (1775-1851) once said to his fellow-artist John Ruskin: "Atmosphere is my style." The Norwegian artist Johan Christian Dahl (1788-1857) indeed gave much importance to the sky, as a part of his landscape painting.

Notes to The Preliminary Notebook

(p. 69) "but the (spoken) tongue, if it is white, would be the opposite of heavily coated." Chappuis alludes here to the notion of "poésie blanche." The poet René Daumal (1908-1944) coined the term in his seminal essay "Poésie noire et poésie blanche" (1954), now available in the paperback gathering, *Le Contre-Ciel* (Gallimard, 1955, 1990). In this essay, Daumal explains the sense of "poésie blanche," literally "white" (but also "blank") poetry, which could paraphrased as "sparse, pure poetry." Such poetry is often fragmentary, seemingly abstract (though not necessarily so when one reads closely).

(p. 73) The French poet Francis Ponge (1899-1988) sometimes published his notes, initial drafts, and textual variants alongside the definitive text, notably in *La Fabrique du Pré* (1971).

(p. 73) The French poet Philippe Jaccottet (b. 1925) has published five volumes of notes: *La Semaison: Carnets 1954-1979* (1984), *La Seconde Semaison: Carnets 1980-1994* (1996), *Carnets 1995-1998: La Semaison, III* (2001), *Observations et autres notes anciennes 1947-1962* (1998), *Taches de soleil, ou d'ombre: Notes sauvegardées 1952-2005* (2013).

(p. 74) Martial de Brives (1600-1653). The phrase *"exhalaisons alambiquées"* can be found in his book *Le Parnasse seraphique, et les derniers soupirs de la Muse* (1660).

(p. 75) Jean Tortel (1904-1993) is a French poet. The "Entretien de Jean Tortel avec Suzanne Nash" was published in *Poésie*, No. 29, 1984, pp. 90-106.

(p. 75) "Gisèle" here is the French artist Gisèle Celan-Lestrange (1927-1991), Paul Celan's wife. Her work was shown in François Ditesheim's gallery, the Galerie Ditesheim, between 18 May and 23 June 1984. This gallery is now called the Ditesheim-Maffei Gallery and located in Neuchâtel, Switzerland.

Notes to A Notebook of Ridges

(p. 85) "Crossing this ridge, whose sheets of schist. . ." "La traverse de cette crête de schiste, dont les feuillets sont verticaux, demande quelques précautions." Robert Touchon, "Massif des Cerces et de la Moulinière," *La Montagne,* March 1910 ; reprinted in *Premiers alpinistes en Clarée (Cerces-Thabor),* edited by René Siestrunck, Éditions Transhumances, 2015, p. 54.

(p. 86) "Yet where there's danger, also grows what can save." Friedrich Hölderlin: "Wo aber Gefahr ist, / wächst das Rettende auch" (from his poem "Patmos," 1803).

(p. 92) "Fire. Its relationship to mountains, to their ridges. . . ." "Le feu. Son rapport à la montagne, à ses crêtes. La montagne comme le souvenir apaisé d'un grand feu." Philippe Jaccottet, *Taches de soleil, ou d'ombre,* Éditions Le Bruit du Temps, 2013, p. 112.

(p. 93) "Beeches, perhaps sorbs. . ." Pierre Chappuis, in *Like Bits of Wind: Selected Poetry and Poetic Prose 1974-2014,* p. 267. "Hêtres, alisiers peut-être / pour scander / l'ondoiement de la crête . . ." (See *Entailles,* Éditions José Corti, 2014, p. 24.)

(p. 97) "Narrow footpaths recall that one side of the mountain. . ." Pierre-Albert Jourdan, *The Straw Sandals: Selected Prose and Poetry,* 2011, Chelsea Editions, p. 49. "De fins sentiers rappellent que les liens ne cessent d'exister d'un versant à l'autre; que les appels sont possibles par-delà cette tranche aiguë, ce long silex déchiqueté, cette énigme" (p. 48).

(p. 101). "Crowned with rank fumiter. . ." William Shakespeare, *King Lear,* Act 4, Scene 4.

(p. 103) "Extending from a gap ripped open from below. . ." "D'une déchirure pratiquée par en-dessous dans l'épaisse couche noyant le pays dépasse, dents tournées vers le haut, une crête hérissée de sapins." Pierre Chappuis, *Un cahier de nuages,* Le feu de nuict, 1989, p. 16.

(p. 103) "A fluttering fan. . ." Matsuo Basho (1644-1694). With thanks to my friends Teiji and Masako Toriyama, who pointed this haiku out to me and helped me to translate it.

(p. 104) *The Little Engine That Could*, Watty Piper, Platt & Munk, 1930. The edition evoked here is that of 1954, with illustrations by George and Doris Hauman.

(p. 106) "Crestfallen. . ." The etymology is not entirely established, but the word, going back to the late sixteenth century, refers to a mammal (especially a horse) or a bird having a fallen or drooping crest. Some etymologists specify that this is the "crest" (head) of a diseased horse, or of a horse with its head on its chest after defeat in a battle. Others point to the drooping crest or comb of a bird, such as a rooster.

(p. 106) "The demon of analogy." Stéphane Mallarmé, "Le Démon de l'analogie," *Divagations* (1897).

(p. 107) "On 19 February 1855, Henry David Thoreau. . ." Thoreau's letter is found in his *Correspondence* (p. 373), as quoted by Mary Elkins Moller in *Thoreau in the Human Community*, University of Massachusetts Press, 1980, pp. 60-61.

(p. 107) "On the ridge, among the blades of wild grass." Pierre-Albert Jourdan, *The Straw Sandals*, Chelsea Editions, 2011, p. 75. "Sur la crête, parmi les herbes" (p. 74).

(p. 108) Languid to the south. . ." Pierre-Albert Jourdan, *The Straw Sandals*, Chelsea Editions, 2011, p. 31. "Alangui au sud, abrupt au nord. / Sur la crête tout est donné" (p. 30).

(p. 108) "Francesco Petrarca, when he climbed. . ." John Taylor, *The Apocalypse Tapestries*, Xenos Books, 2004, p. 41. See Petrarch's *L'Ascension du Mont Ventoux*, translated from the Latin into French by Denis Montebello, Sequences, 1990.

(p. 108) "Along a huge cloud's ridge. . ." John Keats, "Sleep and Poetry" (1816).

(p. 109) "This mountain landscape in which, in the middle of a dark ridge. . ." Philippe Jaccottet, *And, Nonetheless: Selected Prose and Poetry 1990-2009*, Chelsea

NOTES

Editions, 2011, p. 305. "Ce paysage de montagne où, du milieu d'une crête sombre, s'élevait un pic aussi lumineux que s'il eût été une pointe de lance taillée dans le diamant : lumière surnaturelle comme on n'en voit qu'en rêve ; et c'en était un" (p. 304).

(p. 113) In order to get around several serrated formations. . ." "Pour contourner plusieurs dentelures de l'arête, nous descendîmes à droite, sur le versant N.-E., dans un couloir rempli de gros blocs, par lequel nous arrivâmes en quelques instants à un plus grand couloir sur le même versant juste à l'endroit où il plonge vers le bas avec une raideur effrayante." W.A.B. Coolidge, "Cinq nouvelles courses dans l'Oisans en 1891," *Annuaire de la Société des Touristes du Dauphiné*, No. 17, 1891 ; *Premiers alpinistes en Clarée (Cerces-Thabor)*, edited by René Siestrunck, Éditions Transhumances, 2015, p. 23.

(p. 113) "Saint-Beuve forged the image. . ." "La beauté chez lui, même la beauté de la pensée, tient trop à la forme; elle est comme enchaînée à la cime des mots (...) à la *crête* brillante des syllabes." Sainte-Beuve, *Chateaubriand et son groupe littéraire sous l'Empire*, t. 1, 1860, p. 363.

(p. 114) "The pauses or blank spaces. . ." Pierre-Albert Jourdan, *The Straw Sandals: Selected Prose and Poetry*, 2011, Chelsea Editions, p. 131. "L'intervalle, l'espace qui relie les fragments, maximes ou notes où les mots sont, pour reprendre une expression d'Yves Bonnefoy, 'comme la ligne de crête d'un silence'. . ." (p. 130).

(p. 116) "On the ridge of the Mount of Olives. . ." "And David went up by the ascent of the Mount Oliviet, and wept as he went up" (2 Samuel 15:30). See also Matthew 21:1, 26:30, etc.), which shows Jesus on the Mount of Olives and weeping over Jerusalem. Jesus ascended to heaven from the Mount of Olives (Acts 1:9-12).

(p. 116) "Yves Bonnefoy: 'The interruption of the line. . .'" Yves Bonnefoy, "Devant la Saint-Victoire", *Remarques sur le dessin*, Mercure de France, 1993, p. 36.

Notes to The Word and the Stream

(p. 125) La Clarée is a mountain stream found in the Hautes-Alpes region of France, near Montgenèvre and Briançon. It is a tributary of the Durance river.

(p. 132) Hölderlin's "Ein Rätsel ist Reinentsprungenes," from the fourth strophe of the poem "The Rhine," by Friedrich Hölderlin (1770-1843).

(p. 138) *The Pilgrim's Progress from This World, to That Which Is to Come* (1678) is a Christian allegory, written in the form of a dream sequence, by John Bunyan (1628-1688).

Printed in Poland
by Amazon Fulfillment
Poland Sp. z o.o., Wrocław